REPUBLICAN Humor

REPUBLICAN Humor

Edited by

Stephen J. Skubik, C.L.U., and Hal E. Short

Foreword (and 58 stories) by
President Gerald R. Ford

Introduction (and 7 stories) by
Vice President Nelson A. Rockefeller

Published by **ACROPOLIS BOOKS LTD.** • WASHINGTON, D.C. 20009

ACROPOLIS BOOKS LTD.
Colortone Building, 2400 17th St., N.W.
Washington, D.C. 20009

Printed in the United States of America by
COLORTONE PRESS, Creative Graphics Inc.
Washington, D.C. 20009

A copy of our (the Republican National Committee) report is filed with the Federal Election Commission and is available for purchase from the Federal Election Commission, Washington, D.C.

Illustrated by Victor Vashi and Bill Fleishell

Library of Congress Cataloging in Publication Data
Main entry under title:

Republican humor.

    1. American wit and humor.   I. Skubik, Stephen J.   II. Short, Hal E., 1911-
PN6162.R394   817'.5'408   76-6158
ISBN 0-87491-033-1
ISBN 0-87491-034-X pbk.

Foreword
by President Gerald R. Ford

In my remarks to the Congress after being sworn in as our 38th President, I said: "Truth is the glue that holds government together, not only our Government, but civilization as well." I believe this with all my heart.

But government and the political process need not be pompous and unsmiling. The national costume does not have to be a stuffed shirt. Humor can be the lubricant that eases our journey through life.

I have now spent twenty-seven years in American politics and I have seen first-hand the therapeutic effect of a timely or timeless joke. In the words of Kahlil Gibran: "A sense of humor is a sense of proportion."

In politics, a sense of proportion *and* a sense of humor should be written into the job description of every legislator and administrator. Officials who can laugh together can work together. The aisle separating Republicans and Democrats need never be so wide that it can't be bridged by good humor.

Fortunately for all of us in government—federal, state, and local—political humor is alive and well in America. Sometimes the humor is inadvertent. I still feel for the master of ceremonies at a mid-West banquet I attended in 1974. At the conclusion of the program, so that we could keep to our schedule, he asked the audience to keep their seats until the Presidential party had left. But his actual words had a life of their own. He said, "Ladies and gentlemen, this concludes our program but would you please remain in your seats—while the President is removed from the hall!"

Sometimes humor is strangely prophetic. On March 9, 1968, as Minority Leader of the House of Representatives, I was asked to be the Republican speaker at the annual dinner of the Gridiron Club in Washington, D.C. This organization of distinguished journalists and their guests, gets together once a year for a fun evening of political satire and commentary. The audience is so prestigious, a waiter could spill soup in any direction and not miss a celebrity.

In March of 1968, election fever was beginning to spread. Speculation as to who would be the Republican and Democratic nominees for President and Vice President became the unofficial theme of the evening. And so, with tongue firmly planted in cheek, I decided to announce my own intentions. I turned to Hubert Humphrey, who was then Vice President of the United States, and solemnly assured him that I had absolutely no designs on his job.

I then added: "I love the House of Representatives, despite the long, irregular hours. Sometimes, though, when it's late and I'm tired and hungry—on that long drive home to Alexandria—as I go past 1600 Pennsylvania Avenue, I do seem to hear a little voice saying: "If you lived here, you'd be home now.' "

In 1968, I had no inkling of how loud that little voice might get.

I believe in laughter. I look on it as one of the precious gifts that God has given to mankind. I admire, as Walter Scott did, the "wit that loves to play, not wound".

Americans are a diverse people living together in many different styles and places. We are united more by the way we look at things than by the traditional ties of blood or belief or battles long forgotten. And when we are able to look at the brighter side of our troubles, and the lighter side of our struggles, and see the smile that lies just below the surface of our neighbor's face, we Americans are at our very best.

Introduction

Laughter — The Fifth Freedom

Humor is part of the irrepressible spirit of a free people. Only a secure and confident democracy can tolerate the freedom to laugh at its own foibles.

In Washington, a sense of humor becomes an essential part of one's survival kit. Laughter has a marvelous capacity to keep things in perspective in the Nation's Capital—especially egos. Laughing at our own human failings makes us more bearable—to ourselves as well as everyone else. And observing the foibles of friends and adversaries makes our own missteps more tolerable.

In short, the waves of honest laughter won't upset a sturdy ship of state. They just help keep the crew sharp.

NELSON A. ROCKEFELLER
VICE PRESIDENT

Contents

FOREWORD by President Gerald R. Ford v
INTRODUCTION by Vice President Nelson A. Rockefeller vii
Humor of President Ford 13
Humor of Vice President Rockefeller 37
Mary Louise Smith, *Chairman, Republican National Committee* 39
Dean Burch, *Former Chairman, Republican National Committee* 42
Jeremiah Milbank, *Chairman, Republican National Finance
    Committee* 43
Thomas S. Kleppe, *Secretary of Interior* 44
Rogers C. B. Morton, *Counselor to the President* 46
James E. Akins, *U.S. Ambassador to Saudi Arabia* 48
Mark Evans Austad, *U.S. Ambassador to Finland* 49
John Sherman Cooper, *U.S. Ambassador to the German
    Democratic Republic* 51
John A. Volpe, *U.S. Ambassador to Italy* 52
Robert F. Bennett, *Governor of Kansas* 53
Otis R. Bowen, *Governor of Indiana* 54
Mills E. Godwin, Jr., *Governor of Virginia* 55
Jay S. Hammond, *Governor of Alaska* 56
William G. Milliken, *Governor of Michigan* 58
Arch A. Moore, Jr., *Governor of West Virginia* 59
Robert D. Ray, *Governor of Iowa* 61
David F. Cargo, *Former Governor of New Mexico* 62
Warren P. Knowles, *Former Governor of Wisconsin* 64
Ronald Reagan, *Former Governor of California* 65
Earl B. Ruth, *Governor of Samoa Territory* 68
Bill Brock, *U.S. Senator, Tennessee* 69
Carl T. Curtis, *U.S. Senator, Nebraska* 71
Bob Dole, *U.S. Senator, Kansas* 73
Pete V. Domenici, *U.S. Senator, New Mexico* 75
Paul J. Fannin, *U.S. Senator, Arizona* 77
Jake Garn, *U.S. Senator, Utah* 79

Barry Goldwater, *U.S. Senator, Arizona* 81
Roman L. Hruska, *U.S. Senator, Nebraska* 83
Paul Laxalt, *U.S. Senator, Nevada* 85
Charles McC. Mathias, Jr., *U.S. Senator, Maryland* 87
Bob Packwood, *U.S. Senator, Oregon* 88
Charles H. Percy, *U.S. Senator, Illinois* 89
Hugh Scott, *U.S. Senator, Pennsylvania* 90
William L. Scott, *U.S. Senator, Virginia* 92
Robert T. Stafford, *U.S. Senator, Vermont* 93
Robert Taft, Jr., *U.S. Senator, Ohio* 94
Strom Thurmond, *U.S. Senator, South Carolina* 96
John G. Tower, *U.S. Senator, Texas* 99
Bill Archer, *Congressman, Texas* 100
John M. Ashbrook, *Congressman, Ohio* 101
Clarence J. Brown, *Congressman, Ohio* 103
William S. Cohen, *Congressman, Maine* 104
James M. Collins, *Congressman, Texas* 105
Silvio O. Conte, *Congressman, Massachusetts* 106
Edward J. Derwinski, *Congressman, Illinois* 108
Marvin L. Esch, *Congressman, Michigan* 111
Edwin D. Eshelman, *Congressman, Pennsylvania* 112
Paul Findley, *Congressman, Illinois* 113
Gilbert Gude, *Congressman, Maryland* 114
Tennyson Guyer, *Congressman, Ohio* 116
H. John Heinz, III, *Congressman, Pennsylvania* 118
Marjorie S. Holt, *Congresswoman, Maryland* 119
Henry J. Hyde, *Congressman, Illinois* 121
James P. Johnson, *Congressman, Colorado* 122
Robert J. Lagomarsino, *Congressman, California* 123
Robert McClory, *Congressman, Illinois* 124
W. Henson Moore, *Congressman, Louisiana* 125
Carlos J. Moorhead, *Congressman, California* 126
Larry Pressler, *Congressman, South Dakota* 127
John J. Rhodes, *Congressman, Arizona* 128
Matthew J. Rinaldo, *Congressman, New Jersey* 129
Herman T. Schneebeli, *Congressman, Pennsylvania* 131
Richard T. Schulze, *Congressman, Pennsylvania* 132
Keith G. Sebelius, *Congressman, Kansas* 134
Bud Shuster, *Congressman, Pennsylvania* 135
Joe Skubitz, *Congressman, Kansas* 137
Floyd Spence, *Congressman, South Carolina* 139
Alan Steelman, *Congressman, Texas* 140
Steve Symms, *Congressman, Idaho* 142
Gene Taylor, *Congressman, Missouri* 143
Guy Vander Jagt, *Congressman, Michigan* 145

G. William Whitehurst, *Congressman, Virginia* 147
Larry Winn, Jr., *Congressman, Kansas* 148
John W. Wydler, *Congressman, New York* 149
Chalmers P. Wylie, *Congressman, Ohio* 151
C. W. Bill Young, *Congressman, Florida* 152
Don W. Adams, *Republican National Committee, Illinois* 154
Frederick Biebel, *Republican National Committee, Connecticut* 155
Mrs. Harold B. Barton, *Republican National Committee, Kentucky* . . . 157
Mrs. Concepcion C. Barrett, *Republican National Committee, Guam* . . 158
Mrs. Grace Boulton, *Republican National Committee, Oklahoma* 159
Edward Brennan, *Republican National Committee, Hawaii* 160
Mrs. Myrene R. Brewer, *Republican National Committee, Utah* 161
William C. Cramer, *Republican National Committee, Florida* 162
David R. Forward, *Republican National Committee, Maryland* 164
Richard C. Frame, *Republican National Committee, Pennsylvania* . . . 165
Mrs. M. Stanley Ginn, *Republican National Committee, Missouri* 166
John H. Haugh, *Republican National Committee, Arizona* 167
Mrs. James F. Hooper, *Republican National Committee, Mississippi* . . 168
Cyril M. Joly, Jr., *Republican National Committee, Maine* 170
John R. Linnell, *Republican National Committee, Maine* 171
George N. McMath, *Republican National Committee, Virginia* 173
Edwin G. Middleton, *Republican National Committee, Kentucky* 175
Mrs. Isabel C. Moberly, *Republican National Committee, Montana* . . . 176
Mrs. Cynthia Newman, *Republican National Committee, Virginia* . . . 179
Edmund E. Pendleton, *Republican National Committee, District
    of Columbia* 180
Mrs. Elsa Sandstrom, *Republican National Committee, California* . . . 182
Bernard M. Shanley, *Republican National Committee, New Jersey* . . . 184
Mrs. Orriette Sinclair, *Republican National Committee, Idaho* 186
Charles A. Slocum, *Republican National Committee, Minnesota* 188
Mrs. Estelle Stacy Carrier, *Republican National Committee, Wyoming* . 190
ACKNOWLEDGEMENTS 192
INDEX 193

The Humor of President Gerald R. Ford

As Selected From Recent Speeches

FOOTBALL

.... As many of you know, I've always had a great interest in football. I played center for the University of Michigan and I still remember my senior year back in 1934. The Wolverines played Ohio State and we lost 34 to zero. And to make it even worse, that year we lost seven out of our eight games. But what really hurt was when they voted me Their Most Valuable Player—I didn't know whether to smile or sue! ...

Commencement of Ohio State University
Friday, August 30, 1974
Columbus, Ohio

GOLF

I've really enjoyed listening to our eight honorees describe their greatest moments in golf. And if I may, I'd like to tell you the most memorable golfing experience I ever had. I was at that Burning Tree course just outside of Washington when Ben Hogan, Jack Nicklaus and Byron Nelson came up to me and said they were looking for another great golfer to join them—I said, 'Well, here I am!'—And they said, 'Good. You can help us look!'

I didn't mind that so much. But what really hurt was when Arnold Palmer asked me to wear his slacks under an assumed name. . . .

They say you can always tell how good a player is by the number of people in the gallery. You've heard of Arnie's Army? My group is called Ford's Few.

13

I've figured it out. My problem is, I have a very wild swing. I'll tell you how wild my swing is. Back on my home course, they don't yell 'Fore!' They yell, 'Ford!'

You know all those Secret Service men you've seen around me? When I play golf, they get combat pay!'

But I try to keep my hand in whenever I can. Personally, I like to play golf with Henry Kissinger. Henry Kissinger is undoubtedly one of the greatest diplomats the world has ever known. I'll tell you why I say that. Last week I was in a sand trap. There was a water hazard beyond that and then 95 feet to the first hole. And Henry conceded the putt!

But this afternoon, I had one of the greatest thrills of my life. The chance to play a few holes with the super stars of world golfing. I can't tell you how I felt out there surrounded by these legendary names—Berg, Hogan, Nelson, Nicklaus, Palmer, Player, Sarazen, Snead! It was almost like being in Golfer's Heaven!

But as the cliché goes, tonight I have good news and bad news. The good news is that four of our honorees—Jack Nicklaus, Arnold Palmer, Gary Player and Sam Snead—will be competing in the World Open beginning tomorrow. The bad news is, today they shared the course with me—I'll tell you what I mean:

In 1972, I played with Sam Snead in the Pro-Am before the Kemper Open. He didn't go on to win the tournament.

In 1973, I played with Miller Barber before the Kemper Open. And *he* didn't go on to win the tournament.

This year I played with Tom Weiskopf before the Kemper Open—and Dave Stockton before the Pleasant Valley Open. And neither of *them* went on to win the tournaments.

In Washington, I'm known as the President of the United States. In golf, I'm known as the Jinx of the Links!

I figured it out that Snead, Barber, Weiskopf and Stockton blew $165,000 in prize money. If you think they're unhappy, you should see the Internal Revenue Service. . . . .

The Opening of the World Golf Hall of Fame
Wednesday, September 11, 1974
Pinehurst, North Carolina

THE PRESS

. . . Anybody in public life is well aware of how important the judgments of the press are. I'm firmly convinced that if the good

Lord had made the world today, he would have spent six days creating the heavens and earth and all the living creatures upon it. But on the seventh day, He would not have rested—He would have justified it to Helen Thomas. . . .

SEXUAL DISCRIMINATION

. . . But I do appreciate your asking me to be here today on this historic occasion—the inauguration of the first male President of the Washington Press Club. As one President to another, Ron, I salute you. And I also salute the members of the Washington Press Club for breaking down the barriers of sexual discrimination. I'm sure you all know where I stand on this issue. As I prove every morning at breakfast time, I certainly don't believe that a woman's place is in the kitchen.

BATTLE OF THE SEXES

If our country is to survive and prosper, we need the best efforts of all Americans—men and women—to bring it about. And besides, as a great philosopher once said—I think it was Henry Kissinger—nobody will ever win the Battle of the Sexes. There's just too much fraternizing with the enemy.

Washington Press Club
Wednesday, September 18, 1974
Washington, D.C.

DOGS

. . . Leo Thorsness mentioned to me earlier that the hunting season opened here in South Dakota last Saturday—and, by coincidence, you might have seen in the newspapers and on TV, the White House has a new addition. My daughter, Susan, and our White House photographer, Dave Kennerly, got together and surprised me with an eight-month old golden retriever. And I'd like to tell you the story of how Susan and Dave bought this dog.

They called up a very highly recommended kennel and said they wanted to get a golden retriever. The owner of the kennel said fine. Who will the owner be? And they said, it's a surprise—they would like to keep it a secret. Well, the kennel owner said he did not sell dogs that way. He would have to know the dog was going to a good home.

So Susan and Dave assured him that it would be. They

explained that the parents are friendly, middle-aged, and live in a big white house with a fence around it.

The kennel owner said, "Good. Do they own or rent?" Susan and Dave thought a moment, and said, "Well, you might say it's public housing."

The kennel owner said, "Okay. Now this is a big dog who is going to eat a lot. Does the father have a steady job?" Well—there they were stuck for an answer.

Needless to say, they got the dog and, very appropriate to the spirit of the Bicentennial, we have named her Liberty. A reporter asked my daughter Susan who is going to take care of Liberty? Who is going to feed her and groom her and take her out in the morning and at night? And Susan did not hesitate a minute. She said, "Daddy!"

So I have a feeling this is one Liberty that is going to cost me some of mine.

South Dakota Republican State Central Committee Rally
Wednesday, October 16, 1974
Sioux Falls, South Dakota

DANCING

You know, when I saw this grand old ballroom, it brought back so many happy memories of Benny Goodman, Tommy Dorsey and Woody Herman. When Betty and I were courting, we used to go out dancing to the music of these big bands. We had a problem though. Betty had studied modern dance and I was a former football player. She never really came right out and said I was a poor dancer. She's much too kind for that. But she did have a rather interesting theory as to why I played center rather than quarterback. She said it's one of the few positions on a football team where you don't have to move your feet!

Republican Luncheon
Thursday, October 24, 1974
Des Moines, Iowa

REGISTRATION

It's a great pleasure to be here in Chicago again—the home of the Bears, the Bulls, and the kangaroo. That's what I like about Chicago. You can always count on exciting things happening here.

Dan Terra tells me that the way that kangaroo has been dodging tacklers, there's a big controversy over what to do with him when they catch him. The Chicago police want to put him in the zoo—the Chicago Bears want to put him in the backfield—and, of course, the Democrats want to register him—at least once!

Illinois Republican Fundraising Dinner
Thursday, October 24, 1974
Chicago, Illinois

APPROPRIATION

As Chairman of the Subcommittee on Appropriations for State, Justice, Commerce and Judiciary, it's no secret that John Rooney is a man of some consequence around here. You know how Henry Kissinger flew to China in a Boeing 707? One word from John—and he comes back in a Greyhound bus!

Representative John Rooney Reception
Tuesday, November 26, 1974
The State Department

PRESIDENTS

I don't have to tell you I deeply appreciate the opportunity to meet with you tonight, as leaders of commerce and industry, to discuss some very serious economic problems that we all face.

The mutuality of our problems was never more clearly stated than when I was introduced at a business conference quite recently. The moderator said, "The greatness of America is that anyone can grow up to be president of an auto company, president of an airline, president of a utility, or President of the United States." Then he took a long pause and added, "That's just one of the chances they have to take!"

Business Council
Wednesday, December 11, 1974
Mayflower Hotel

BOY SCOUTS

They say once a Scout always a Scout, and I can tell you from my own experience that is true. After all these years I still love the outdoors. I still know how to cook for myself, at least breakfast.

And as anyone who saw those pictures of me in Japan will know, on occasion I still go around in short pants.

Scouter of the Year Banquet
Monday, December 2, 1974
Washington, D. C.

FOOTBALL

I'm sure I don't have to tell any of you the problems of being an Athletic Director or Head Coach. For instance, I see my good friend Bear Bryant sitting here . . . I was talking to Bear and he said we both had the very same experience on New Year's Day. I said, 'How is that possible? I was skiing and you were at the Orange Bowl.' He said, 'That's what I mean. We both hit the top—and after that, it was all down hill!

National Collegiate Athletics Association
Tuesday, January 7, 1975
Washington, D.C.

DIFFERENT VIEW

Let me thank Chris Schenkel for that fine introduction. You know, since I became President, I'm usually introduced in a very stately and dignified manner—such as tonight. But there was one dinner when I was introduced by a former teammate of mine from my old Michigan football team—and I'll never forget that introduction. He said, "Ladies and Gentlemen, it might interest you to know that I played football with Jerry Ford for two years—and it made a lasting impression on me. I was quarterback. Jerry Ford was the center. And you might say, it gave me a completely different view of the President!

HOWARD COSELL

If you stop to think about it, there are many similarities between football and government. For instance, in both areas nothing is ever done without discussing it first. In football, it's called a huddle. In Washington, it's called a debate. And sometimes the talk goes on for many, many hours without really saying anything. In Washington, it's called a filibuster. In football, it's called Howard Cosell.

Howard Cosell takes a lot of kidding, but in all fairness,

18

someone once said: "To me, Howard Cosell will always look ten feet tall!" I don't know *who* said it . . . . I think it was Abe Beame.

WOODY HAYES

It is a real honor to be here tonight because football has meant so much to me through the years. You might be interested to know that I have even put together a small collection of memorable football quotations and I would like to share two of them with you tonight. The first quotation is from Grantland Rice: "When the one great scorer comes to write against your name—he marks—not that you won or lost—but how you played the game." And the other is from Woody Hayes: "Bah! Humbug!

Incidentally, I wish Woody Hayes and the Ohio State Buckeyes good luck in the Rose Bowl. But as a former Michigan football player and as a twelve-term Congressman from Michigan, I think that's about as far as I should go. I may cook my own breakfast but I'm not about to cook my own goose!

Remarks by Gerald R. Ford in Presenting
the National Football Foundation and Hall of Fame's
Distinguished American Award to Bob Hope
December 10, 1974

FOOTBALL

I also appreciate this opportunity to be here because, as a former assistant football coach—I not only know your problems and concerns, but I've lived them. I'll never forget the time back at Yale when I went to a movie theatre with our great head coach, Ducky Pond—and the movie just happened to be that film classic King Kong.

Well, who can ever forget that final scene? King Kong is standing on top of the Empire State Building and men are shouting at him; women are screaming at him; the police are shooting at him; even airplanes are firing machine guns at him.

I was so impressed, I leaned over to Ducky Pond and whispered, 'When was the last time you ever saw anything like that?' Ducky said, 'Tuesday. I had a meeting with the alumni association!'

As a resident of Washington, I want you to know what a thrill it is having you all here. Washington is a real football town and you can't imagine the excitement seeing John McKay fly in over the Potomac; Ara Parseghian drive in over the Potomac; and Bear Bryant walk in over the Potomac.

You know, sometimes I wonder why we don't talk more about the history of our sport. Football is a very old and honorable game. It was played by the ancient Chinese, the Greeks and the Romans. In fact, many ancient peoples played a form of football just to keep warm in the winter. And it still works. I saw Woody Hayes after the Rose Bowl . . . boy, was he steamed!

No, I'm only kidding. You all know where my loyalties are but I firmly believe that on New Year's Day, two of the finest football teams in America today were involved in the Rose Bowl. The University of Southern California playing it—and the University of Michigan watching it—on TV.

Seriously, I think both Woody Hayes and John McKay did a superlative job and if they ever want to come over to the White House for breakfast, I'll personally fix them both the breakfast of champions.

The American Football Coaches Association Dinner
Thursday, January 9, 1975
Washington, D.C.

TELEPHONE

I'm very grateful for this very unusual gift—a lamp made out of a phone. But I have to tell you, I'm a little worried about it. I'm in enough trouble now without saying to someone 'Excuse me. I have to answer the lamp!'

Someone just told me that the lamp works but the phone doesn't. That's all right. Maybe that's what we need these days—more light and less talk.

Industrial Payroll Savings Committee
Response to Gift of Phone-Lamp
Thursday, January 16, 1975
Washington, D.C.

PRESIDENTS

Let me thank you for asking me to be a part of this very auspicious occasion . . .

I'm sure Bill Broom will make an excellent President. And believe me, it isn't easy being President. They ask impossible things of you. First they take away your swimming pool—and then they

20

want you to come clean.

National Press Club—Swearing-in of new President
Sunday, January 26, 1975
Washington, D.C.

PRESIDENTIAL CANDIDATES

Let me say how much I enjoyed the magnificent voice of Miss Barbara Shuttleworth. Miss Shuttleworth, you are a pleasure to the ear and to the eye as well. My only disappointment is that you didn't sing my favorite song. The one that's dedicated to all the Democratic candidates for President. Maybe you know it. It's called—'I love a Parade!'

I love the name of the Alfalfa Club. For the benefit of those who may be attending this dinner for the first time, let me explain how the Alfalfa Club came to be called that. It was named after the plant that sends its roots down the deepest for liquid refreshment. I don't know what liquid it's looking for—but this year—it better be oil!

That is one thing Scoop Jackson and I agree on. If we don't solve the oil problem—come 1995, Boeing is going to be making roller skates!

One of the things I've always liked about the Alfalfa Club— we've never lost our sense of humor. I know we haven't lost our sense of humor just by looking at the time schedule they gave me for this dinner. It has items like: 8:18—serve entree. 8:35—remove plates. 8:40 serve salad. But the item that really proved we haven't lost our sense of humor, it this: 9:50—candidate's acceptance speech. President Hubert Humphrey responds—*briefly.*

Gentlemen—Senator Humphrey is a dear friend of mine and I can still remember the very first time I ever heard him speak at the Alfalfa Club. Hubert was in the second hour—of a five minute talk . . .

I couldn't find my program, so I leaned over to the member sitting next to me and asked, 'What follows Senator Humphrey?' He looked at his watch, then he looked at me and said, 'Christmas!'

Now for those of you who might be a little confused by my referring to Hubert as President Humphrey—let me explain this in a very clear and concise way:

Hubert Humphrey is the President of the Alfalfa Club and I am a member of the Alfalfa Club. I am also President of the United

21

States. Now I have never been President of the Alfalfa Club but Hubert was Vice President of the United States when I was Minority Leader of the House.

Then President Humphrey—and as I explained, this is President of the Alfalfa Club, as differentiated from George Bush, who is running for President of the United States on the Alfalfa ticket—President Humphrey ran for President of the United States while I ran for Congress—not knowing that I would some day be Vice President of the United States, but not of the Alfalfa Club—at the same time President Humphrey, of the Alfalfa Club, who was now Senator Humphrey of Minnesota—our former Vice President and candidate for President—would shortly be known, and justifiably so, as Alfalfa's greatest future former Vice President.

You might be interested to know, that in my spare time, I also write the instructions for the income tax.

National Press Club—Swearing-in of new President
Sunday, January 26, 1975
Washington, D.C.

BUDGET

I was reminded before coming here this morning, that I was following in the footsteps of another President who also wanted to present his budget proposals, face to face. The President was Harry Truman and the last such occasion was on January 19th, 1952, when he held a press conference to discuss the budget for the fiscal year 1953. A budget, I might add, that jumped to $85 billion—which was then described as astronomical.

In describing it, President Truman said, "This budget has been the biggest headache I have ever had!" Well, as I look at the budget for the fiscal year 1976, I can only say, "Harry, I hope you left some aspirin for me."

Budget Press Briefing
Saturday, February 1, 1975
Washington, D.C.

KANSAS

Ever since I was a youngster, I have had a special feeling for Kansas—because Kansas is where Dorothy lived before she went to visit the wonderful land of Oz—where all kinds of strange, whimsical and unexpected things happened. But I'm beginning to think that if strange, whimsical and unexpected things were what Dorothy was really interested in, she wouldn't have gone to Oz. She would have come to Washington.

Joint Session of the Kansas State Legislature
Monday, February 10, 1975
State Capitol, Topeka, Kansas

FOOTBALL

As center of the 1934 Michigan football team that lost seven out of its eight season games—five by shutouts—it gives me great personal satisfaction to be elected to the International Churchmen's Sports Hall of Fame. Frankly, as individuals, we were God-fearing—but as a team, we didn't have a prayer.

Letter to: International Churchmen's
Sports Hall of Fame, Inc.
Tuesday, February 11, 1975
Tullahoma, Tennessee

BOB HOPE

Bob, first let me say this luncheon has presented me with some very good news and at the same time some very bad news. The good news, of course, is that my very good friend, Bob Hope, has been named Comedian of the Century, and Bob, I congratulate you for it.

Now, the bad news. How am I ever going to explain this to Earl Butz?

Of course, Bob has received a great many honors during his lifetime and deservedly so. In fact, Bob was telling me just last week he received a very special award from a leading student organization, a very special award. They named Bob the George Carlin of the Stone Age.

Bob, I do want to thank you for this constant dedication on your part to humanitarian causes. Just look at what Bob is doing here in Washington, Not only is he getting this award from this great organization, but later on he is going over to entertain our fighting forces—in the Congress.

National Entertainment Conference
Wednesday, February 12, 1975
Washington, D.C.

SAM DEVINE

Sam Devine has had a rather unique career. He was an F.B.I. agent, a prosecutor—and also a football referee. Which can be a devastating combination. When he called a penalty, you could either lose five yards or five years.

Testimonial For Congressman Sam Devine
February 14, 1975

UNIVERSITY OF MICHIGAN

I'm really looking forward to seeing the program tonight, and I do appreciate the honor of your calling it: THIS IS YOUR UNIVERSITY, MR. PRESIDENT. All I can tell you is, they sure didn't know it back in 1935.

I can still remember spending a good part of my sophomore and junior years washing dishes in the Deke house. And I mean washing dishes. I washed so many dishes I was the only athlete in Michigan history who ever had football knee and dishpan hands at the same time!

So many fine memories come to mind. In my freshman year, I had a job at the University Hospital. I was a waiter in the interns' dining room and the nurses' cafeteria—and it couldn't have been better. I worked in the interns' dining room for *their* benefit—and in the nurses' cafeteria for *mine.*

Personally, I'm intrigued by the differences between then and now—as well as the similarities. For instance, back in Ann Arbor, I lived on the fourth floor of a rooming house and my rent was four dollars. Today, in Washington, that building would be described as a townhouse—the room would be called a pad—the rent would be four hundred dollars—and you still wouldn't get enough hot water!

Of course, that doesn't apply to where I live now. . . . I've only been there seven months and you can't *believe* all the hot water I've gotten into!

Frankly, I just wish some of my critics could have been here tonight. I would have liked them to know what my major was——— economics! It shows you how little times have changed. In 1935, I got my first degree———and in 1975 I'm getting the third degree—and it's still in economics!

A rare night like this allows us to look back—with affection, and at times, with amusement. But our sights should always be set on tomorrow—and the many tomorrows that follow.

24

I know mine are. I tend to follow the sentiments expressed in one of our dearly loved college songs. The one that says: 'I WANT TO GO BACK TO MICHIGAN.' And I do. But with your permission, I would like to do it in 1981.

University of Michigan Club's 23rd Annual Congressional Dinner
Wednesday, March 5, 1975
Washington, D.C.

PRESIDENTIAL CANDIDATES

I couldn't help but notice that Mary Louise Smith has been spending more and more of her time talking to large groups like this. Then again, her counterpart—Bob Strauss, the Democratic National Chairman—has been spending more and more of *his* time talking to large groups—not audiences, candidates for President.

Republican National Committee Leadership Conference Dinner
Friday, March 7, 1975
Washington, D.C.

YALE

I am in very good company welcoming Carla into the Cabinet as Secretary of Housing and Urban Development. Carla, Mr. Justice White—who is about to administer the oath—HUD Under Secretary Jim Mitchell and I are all graduates of Yale Law School.

Maybe I better not say that too loudly. I can imagine a dozen other prospects starting to practice the Wiffenpoof Song.

Swearing-in Ceremony of Carla A. Hills
as Secretary of HUD
Monday, March 10, 1975
Washington, D.C.

BOB HOPE

I have only one thing to say about a program that calls for *me* to follow Bob Hope: Who arranged this? Scoop Jackson?

Radio and Television Correspondent's Assoc.
Annual Dinner
Thursday, March 13, 1975
Washington, D.C.

TV NEWSCASTERS

Before I begin, let me ask you to join with me in a short, but rather solemn ceremony. When I give the signal—would all the TV newscasters in the room please stand—face toward Ron Nessen, and repeat after me: 'There, but for the grace of God, go I!'

I am very honored to be here because, as we all know, there are only three major vehicles to keep us informed as to what is going on in Washington: the electronic media, the print media, and Doonesbury . . . . not necessarily in that order.

Radio and Television Correspondent's Assoc.
Annual Dinner
Thursday, March 13, 1975
Washington, D.C.

KISSINGER

I'm very sorry Secretary Kissinger couldn't be here. I always enjoy listening to Henry. He's so calm, so relaxed, so self-possessed. Henry is the only man I know who can give a press conference and have his shoes shined at the same time.

PRESIDENTIAL CANDIDATES

I want you to know that I listened with great interest—and I might add, great sympathy, to my good friend, Democratic National Committee Chairman, Bob Strauss. I think Bob did the best anybody could for a Party that's suffering from the Domino Theory—but in reverse. The minute one candidate stands up—six more follow him.

But I am sorry Bob Strauss didn't answer the one burning political question that's really on everybody's mind tonight: 'Has Moe Udall's campaign for President peaked too soon?

I want to congratulate Scoop Jackson and all those other Democratic candidates running along with him. The ones with the high hopes and the low profiles.

Obviously, Senator Jackson has many advantages. With a name like Scoop, at least he has the Howard Johnson vote.

But when it comes to the White House, let me extend a sincere welcome to all the Democratic candidates who want to get in on the ground floor. You have my promise that I'll do everything possible to help them get into the White House—on the ground floor. As long as I stay on the second.

Annual Gridiron Dinner
Saturday, March 22, 1975
Washington, D.C.

ALASKA

Let me thank Ted Stevens, the distinguished Senator from Alaska, for that very kind introduction. Personally, I have always felt a very special affinity for the great state of Alaska because there is something about Alaska's weather that always makes me a bit nostalgic. Alaska's weather always reminds me of all the Democrats who used to say: "It'll be a cold day when Jerry Ford becomes President!"

Well—I might just keep this cold wave going a little longer than they think.

PRESIDENTIAL CANDIDATES

Incidentally, you may be interested to know that another one of the Democratic candidates is getting ready to give up the race. I won't say who but yesterday he told Bob Strauss, the Democratic National Chairman, 'I'm getting very discouraged.' And Bob Strauss is such an optimist, he said, 'Why?' The candidate said, 'Why? I'll tell you why. In the last Gallup Poll, 1500 votes were cast and I got thirteen.' Bob said, 'This is no time to get superstitious!'

FUND RAISING

It is a great pleasure to be here tonight and in the spirit of the times, let me welcome you to the Republican Party's first no-frills, economy, $1,000 a plate dinner . . . Thinking positively—how often can you go home from a dinner and realize that every carrot you left on your plate cost you $14.75.

Republican Senate-House Dinner
Tuesday, April 15, 1975
Washington, D.C.

U.S. NAVY

They say the Navy offers opportunity and you better believe it. In 1942, I became an Ensign. In 1943, I became a Lieutenant. In 1945, I became a Lt. Commander. And in 1974, I became Commander-in-Chief. Now, you can't ask for any more opportunity than that.

73rd Annual Navy League Convention
Wednesday, April 23, 1975
New Orleans, Louisiana

POLITICIAN

Let me commend and congratulate Don Johnson, a very extraordinary and gifted artist, for this fine portrait. I like it very much. I like the pose in particular. As a fiscal conservative, I always enjoy seeing a politician with his hand in his *own* pocket!

Gerald R. Ford Portrait Unveiling
at the Capitol Hill Club
Thursday, April 24, 1975
Washington, D.C.

YALE

It is a great pleasure—and a great honor—to be at the Yale Law School's Sesquicentennial Convocation. And I defy *anyone* to say that and chew gum at the same time!

Yale Law School
Friday, April 25, 1975
New Haven, Connecticut

EX-CONGRESSMEN

It is a great treat to be here at this Fifth Annual Alumni gathering of the Former Members of Congress. This is one organization whose members really have it made. You can sleep late each morning; get up when you feel like it; listen to the birds sing; linger over your coffee; spend two hours reading the newspaper—but that isn't the best part. The best part is when you can look up from the newspaper, turn to your wife, and complain about the mess they're making in Washington!

Former Members of Congress Reception
Thursday, May 22, 1975
Washington, D.C.

RAQUEL WELCH

On March 26 of this year, at the White House Ceremony, I had the very great honor to present the American Cancer Society's award to one of the outstanding members of this graduating class, the captain of the Army's football team, Cadet Robert E. Johnson.

. . . I thought you might be interested in something that happened after the White House ceremony. When it was over, Bob Johnson and Homer Smith—Army's distinguished head football

28

coach—had lunch at the White House with a few of the other participants in the ceremony.

Homer Smith found himself sitting beside someone whom he later described as "this nice looking girl," but he didn't know her name. So Homer leaned over and asked her. She said "Raquel." He said, "Raquel? What is your last name?" She said, "Welch."

Now, if you are wondering how anyone could describe Raquel Welch as just a nice looking girl—I think you have to understand the very special philosophy of football coaches. I know, because a long time ago I was one myself. To a football coach real beauty is anyone who is 6 feet 5, weighs 260 pounds and has no front teeth.

1975 Graduation Exercises of West Point Military Academy
Wednesday, June 4, 1975
West Point, New York

PUBLIC SPEAKING

You might be interested to know that my daughter, Susan, gave me some very specific advice on this speech. She asked me not to talk too long, not to tell any jokes, not to talk about her and not to talk about the way things were when I was your age. . . . So, in conclusion.

Holton Arms School Commencement Exercises
Thursday, June 5, 1975
Bethesda, Maryland

SENIOR PROM

It's a pleasure to welcome you to the White House this afternoon. I just wish my daughter Susan could have been here today. I know she would have loved meeting and talking with you all, but she's out in Yosemite studying photography.

Susan graduated from high school last week and, since most of you are now entering your own senior year, I think you might be interested to know where her senior class decided to hold its prom—right here in the White House—while Betty and I were in Europe. . . . I'm sure that was entirely coincidental.

Now holding a prom in the White House may sound like a pretty super idea, but it did create one small problem. The headmaster of the school told me he received a very concerned phone call from the parents of one of the girls. They said, in a quite serious manner, that they make it a practice never to allow their daughter to attend a party in anyone's home when the parents are away. . . . But in this case, they were going to make an exception . . .

Greetings to Students Representing The National
Rural Electric Cooperative Association
Wednesday, June 11, 1975
Washington, D.C.

SMALL BUSINESSMAN

I welcome this opportunity to be here today—to exchange views and feelings with this distinquished cross-section of what has come to be known as the small business community. Personally, I've always been a little amused by that term 'small businessman'—and a few years ago, after a meeting like this, I asked one of the speakers what his definition of a big businessman would be. He said, 'Congressman, it's very simple. A *big* businessman is what a *small* businessman would be if the government would ever let him alone!

Washington Conference of the National Federation of
Independent Business
Tuesday, June 17, 1975
Washington, D.C.

U.S. TREASURY

I appreciate the opportunity to meet with you today as part of the Ohio River Valley White House Conference. As you have already heard from other speakers, there are answers to our many problems—but no easy answers.

The closest we've ever come to an easy answer was the day Secretary Simon took Vice President Rockefeller through the Treasury . . . As they came to the end of the tour, Bill Simon said, "The Treasury is one of the most important aspects of our economic policy." Vice President Rockefeller said, "I'll buy that!" . . . And Simon said, "Sold!"

Ohio River Valley White House Conference
Wednesday, July 2, 1975
Cincinnati, Ohio

MUSIC

I think it is a help when the complex problems we all deal with are at least recognized in part by others, and sometimes this happens in very strange ways.

Two weeks ago, I went back to my hometown of Grand Rapids, Michigan, for a rally in a tremendous college field house. And just as I was coming into the building, I heard the master of ceremonies ask the marching band to play one more selection, something that would be appropriate for the President of the United States. So they played "Nobody Knows the Troubles I've Seen."

National Association of Realtors
November 14, 1974
Las Vegas, Nevada

BOB HOPE

I miss sharing this evening with so many of my good friends and golfing partners—like Bob Hope. I've played with Bob a number of times and Bob has to be the most determined golfer who ever lived. He'll do anything to win. Bob Hope is the only man I know who would take you to see "Jaws" before playing a water hole.

Film Message to the "All American Collegiate
Golf Foundation Dinner" (Waldorf-Astoria Hotel)
Thursday, July 24, 1975
New York, New York

'RIP' WHALEN

In a New York Times interview, I said that when Michigan played Northwestern back in 1934, I knocked 'Rip' Whalen all over the field. I understand that as 'Rip' recalls it, in the second half, he knocked me all over the field. That's the problem with all us old football players. We don't exaggerate. We just remember big.

Letter to Ed Whalen Upon His Receiving the
Distinquished Citizens Award of the National
Football Foundation & Hall of Fame
Monday, July 28, 1975
Chicago, Illinois

DAVID MATHEWS

I have come here today to swear in David Mathews as the new Secretary of HEW.

In Sunday's *Washington Post* I read an article about David

Mathews, and in this one piece alone he was described as innovative, captivating, exceptional, persuasive, gifted and brilliant, and a man of Presidential stature.

Nevertheless, I have still come here today to swear David Mathews in as the new Secretary of HEW.

Swearing-in Ceremony of Secretary of HEW,
Dr. Forrest David Mathews
Friday, August 8, 1975
Washington, D.C.

COMMUNICATION

Because of the emphasis on questions and answers, rather than speeches, I am certain this Conference will be long-remembered in the history of verbal communication. It has been said that a dialogue is when you exchange views with a colleague—and a monologue is when a politician exchanges views with *you.*

The White House Conference
Tuesday, August 19, 1975
Peoria, Illinois

HOT AIR

Let me also reassure you that I will make these remarks short and to the point. If there's one thing Iowa doesn't need in August, it's more hot air.

Iowa State Fair
Monday, August 18, 1975
Des Moines, Iowa

HARDWARE STORE

It is a special pleasure to be here this morning to pay tribute to the American hardware industry. Yours is an industry that has taken American ingenuity and coupled it with some of the most effective merchandising techniques known to mortal man. Now that may seem like exaggeration—but a hardware store is the only business I know of, where you can go to buy a ten-cent carriage bolt—and come out with a can of paint, a new improved screwdriver, 50 pounds of charcoal briquets, a bicycle tire repair kit, 10 minutes worth of free advice, 12 picture hooks, 6 fuses and a lawn mower—and then have to go back because you forgot the ten-cent carriage bolt you went in to buy in the first place!

I've been a typical homeowner most of my life and my wife Betty knows it. She says that sending me to a hardware store is the nearest thing she knows to playing Chicken with our life savings.

Nevertheless, on behalf of all us do-it-yourselfers, let me thank all of you here for making possible that wonder of wonders—the neighborhood hardware emporium—more affectionately known as the world's only candy store for grown-ups.

The Hardware Industry Conference
Monday, August 25, 1975
Chicago, Illinois

COMMUNICATION

As you know, many of you I am sure, I have been a part of the Federal Government for 26 years and I am very concerned about the ever widening communications gap between Washington on our East Coast and our fellow Americans in all other parts of the United States. Too many Americans have difficulty making their views and their wishes known to the people with whom they must communicate in Washington. This difficulty was probably best summed up on an envelope that I received quite recently. It was plaintively addressed: To President Gerald R. Ford, or Vice President Nelson Rockefeller, or Secretary of State Henry Kissinger, or just plain anybody who will listen.

White House Conference—Question and Answer Session
Thursday, September 4, 1975
Seattle, Washington

ANSWERS

Mr. Reed, Governor Brown, Lieutenant Governor Dymally, Stuart Davis, members of the Host Committee, ladies and gentlemen:

This has been a week that I will long remember with great satisfaction, a week that found Dr. Kissinger returning to Washington with some important answers to a very critical situation in the Middle East.

I believe, and believe very, very strongly, that all Americans can take pride in his—and our Nation's—continued and now successful efforts to bring peace to an area of the world that has known so little of it in the last quarter century.

Dr. Kissinger's ability to come up with good answers comes as no surprise to me. In July, when we were in Europe, I visited one of our military bases in Germany, and during the tour of this military installation, I picked up a copy of *Stars and Stripes,* the service newspaper that some of you have read while you were in the service or touring in any of our installations on a worldwide basis.

The next morning, I was looking through it as I was having breakfast and saw a column about contestants in the Miss Universe contest.

On a questionnaire, they were asked to name the greatest person in the world today, and 50 percent of the Miss Universe contestants who answered said Henry Kissinger.

Then I looked very carefully through the rest of the story and couldn't see my name mentioned at all.

So, I circled the story and asked a staff member to take it down the hall to Secretary Kissinger and to ask Henry—one of my most astute advisers—why 50 percent of the most beautiful women in the world had voted for him and I didn't even get a mention.

The aide walked down the hall, showed the story to Henry, who was eating breakfast, and repeated my question.

For a long while Henry didn't say anything, he just sort of kept looking at the story and smiling somewhat self-contentedly to himself.

So, my aide, who had been waiting for Dr. Kissinger's answer, cleared his throat and said, "What should I tell the President?" Henry said, "Tell him to just eat his heart out."

Host Breakfast—Community Convention Center
Friday, September 5, 1975
Sacramento, California

FORD-MUSTANG

Just before I left Washington yesterday morning I received a bit of very good news. Bill Clements, our Deputy Secretary of Defense, as well as the former chairman of Southern Methodist University's Board of Governors, informed me that I had been named the first honorary member of your sensational Mustang Band. All I can say is: I have always been proud to be a Ford. In the future, I will be even more proud to be a Ford Mustang.

Southern Methodist University
Saturday, September 13, 1975
Dallas, Texas

SURFING

I have been looking forward to visiting the campus here at Malibu. Some of you may know, I like skiing and swimming, and here in Malibu one of the big things is surfing, which combines a little of both. Skiing when you do it right and swimming when you do it wrong.

But, I never realized how popular surfing really is until just before the program when I asked President Bill Banowsky how many minutes he wanted me to speak, and Bill just said, "Mr. President, hang 10."

Pepperdine University—Dedication Ceremony For
Firestone Fieldhouse
Saturday, September 20, 1975
Malibu, California

NORMAN LEVINE

President Levine is a very rare and a very unique gentleman, and there is a story behind that compliment.

A few years ago, I shared a head table at a dinner in New York City with Norman Levine. A few people were good enough to ask me to sign their programs, and in so doing, my pen ran out of ink. So, I borrowed Norm's. Well, a few years went by and the next time I saw Norm was in March of this year, when he came to the Oval Office to ask if I would attend this dinner.

After the meeting was over, I asked Norm to accept a pair of cufflinks as a souvenir of his visit to the Oval Office. Norm was very gracious about it. He thanked me, but declined the offer and said—if I didn't mind he'd just like his pen back.

So, I gave Norm a pen and that is why I say he is a very rare and unique gentleman. How often do you meet anyone who ever got something *back* from Washington?

National Association of Life Underwriters Annual Convention
Disneyland Hotel Convention Center
Sunday, September 21, 1975
Anaheim, California

GIN RUMMY

It is always a pleasure to see so many old friends and some new friends again and, in particular, to visit with my very good friend, Bob Georgine.

Bob is well-known as a man of outstanding accomplishments, a demonstrated leader, an exceptional administrator, a concerned citizen and a celebrated gin rummy player.

I say a celebrated gin rummy player but perhaps I'd better explain that term. Bob doesn't celebrate, his opponents do.

As a friend I won't say how good a gin rummy player Bob Georgine is, but two more games and you could have a brand new name—the AFL-CIO-IOU.

AFL-CIO Building and Trades Department
Annual Convention
Monday, September 22, 1975
San Francisco, California

Nelson A. Rockefeller
Vice President

FORD FOUNDATION

My becoming Vice President was made possible by a grant from the Ford Foundation.

THE WHITE HOUSE

My selection by President Ford as his Vice President certainly proved one thing—the White House is an equal opportunity employer.

REPUBLICAN PARTY

I am always delighted when the President asks me to go somewhere to represent the Republican Party. I never had much luck doing that on my own.

RESPONSIBILITIES

The President said he intended to assign me important responsibilities. In fact, he said he was willing to make me responsible for inflation and recession.

"MR. PRESIDENT"

The best part about being Vice President is presiding over the Senate. Where else could I have Barry Goldwater addressing me as "Mr. President."

CIA

When I chaired the Commission investigating the CIA, we asked the witnesses to give the whole truth, nothing but the truth and to speak directly into the flower vase.

ENERGY CRISIS

As a result of the energy crisis, I am trying to stick scrupulously to the 55 miles per hour speed limit. And, I want to tell you, that's quite a stunt in Air Force Two.

Mary Louise Smith
Chairman, Republican National Committee

EMANCIPATION PROCLAMATION

While politics is certainly serious business, I hope there never comes a time when those of us involved in the political arena lose the ability to laugh at ourselves. President Abraham Lincoln, noted for his very dry, sharp wit, knew the value of maintaining a sense of humor. During a critical time for the Union, with the outcome of the war in serious doubt, the President called his cabinet to a meeting at the White House. There he read a chapter from a book by Artemus Ward to them, which he said was very funny. None of the Cabinet as much as smiled, and some considered leaving. The President put the book aside and heaved a long sigh and said, "Gentlemen, why don't you laugh? With the fearful strain that is upon me night and day, if I did not laugh I should die, and you need this medicine as much as I do." Whereupon he came to the reason he had called the Cabinet together. He had wanted the Cabinet to be the first to hear his Emancipation Proclamation.

PRESS INTERVIEWS

Being the first woman chairman of the Republican National Committee has certainly had its unique aspects. Initially, I was referred to as the grandmother from Iowa and the length of my skirt seemed to be more important than my political opinions. I can remember those early press interviews vividly. I spent a considerable amount of time boning up on the vital issues of the day hoping to be well versed and articulate on the many difficult questions I expected to encounter. Sure enough, the questions were even more wide ranging than I had dreamed. They asked me whether I took vitamins.

I didn't at the time but I decided if it was that important maybe I should. They asked me whether I had ever considered dying my grey hair and they asked me if I bought my clothes off the rack. But perhaps the most in-depth question came the day I was asked my measurements. I couldn't help but wonder—when was the last time Bob Strauss or George Bush were asked their measurements?

FRIENDS

But all politicians have their problems to face. I think of the story Tom Milligan, Republican State Chairman of Indiana, tells of former U.S. Senator Jim Watson from Indiana who served during the difficult prohibition era. The Senator, it seems, took a unique position on the prohibition issue. As he used to say, "Some of my friends drink and some of my friends don't drink. And believe me, I'm for my friends."

PSYCHIATRIST

In order to surmount problems, politicians must often rely on imagination. We can take a lesson from the Washington psychiatrist who upon seeing a patient for the first time took him into his office and asked him to relax on the nearby couch. The psychiatrist decided to guage the new patient's state of mind through some simple reaction questions. "Mr. Johnson," the psychiatrist asked, "If you saw a battleship coming down Pennsylvania Avenue, what would you do?" The man thought for a moment and answered, "Well, I guess I would just torpedo it." The psychiatrist was somewhat taken aback but continued the conversation. "Mr. Johnson, where would you get the torpedos?" A slight grin came over the man's face, "Why the same place you'd get the battleship, Doc."

GREAT AMERICANS

But finally there comes a time in every politician's life when we're all brought back to earth. I remember going to a Republican meeting one evening with my husband where I was given one of the most lavish introductions I had ever received. The kind gentleman introducing me went on for a considerable period of time and among other things was very flattering in referring to me as a "great American." Later in the evening as we returned home, I was still elated from the magnanimous words I had heard earlier. I turned to my husband and asked, "Elmer, how many great Americans do you think there really are? He looked at me quizzically and said, "Mary Louise—one less than you think."

Dean Burch
Former Chairman, Republican National Committee

GOLDY BEARWATER

My favorite story from the 1964 presidential campaign involves a speech by Senator Goldwater somewhere in the midwest and, frankly, I don't recall the exact location. The master of ceremonies at this particular event was a middle-aged woman, terribly thrilled over the honor of introducing, in her words, "the next President of the United States." After a suitable peroration, during which she was noticeably nervous and excited, she reached a dramatic climax by stating, "Ladies and Gentlemen, the next President of the United States . . . Goldy Bearwater.

Honey, here's five hundred dollars worth of my thousand dollar plate dinner, I couldn't eat it all."

Jeremiah Milbank
Finance Chairman
Republican National Committee

BAD LUCK

As one who has both won and lost in political contests, I would probably have to go along with the story of the congressman who must have set some kind of a record for bad luck.

Within the short space of a week, he cast two votes against programs which were strongly supported within his district. While he was out on the campaign trail explaining these votes, his home burned to the ground. Then came the crusher: As he listened to early election returns in his hotel room, it became apparent that he was overwhelmingly defeated. He rushed from his room to make a concession speech over the local television station. The elevator fell and, by the time he regained consciousness, he was in the hospital with a broken leg and arm and sundry bruises and abrasions.

His manager called at the hospital with the intention of breaking the news that there would be a $35,000 campaign deficit. Seeing the poor man in traction, he thought that a note of compassion would be more in order.

"Are you suffering much pain?" he asked, with as much sympathy as a deficit-plagued campaign manager could be expected to muster. "Are you hurting as much as you seem to be?"

The shattered statesman was equal to the challenge.

"Only," he moaned "only when I laugh."

CHIN UP

Rogers C. B. Morton, former cabinet member and Congressman, and one of my predecessors as Secretary of the Interior, was brought up in Kentucky horse country.

While campaigning in Louisville one day for his brother, Thruston, Rog spotted an unshaven and seedy-looking old gentleman on a street corner. Being a generous man, Rog handed the man a dollar and said, "Chin up."

Morton passed the same corner the next day, the same old timer handed him a ten-dollar bill and whispered: "Good pick, Buddy. Chin Up paid nine-to-one."

ADVERTISING

A smalltown storekeeper inherited a sizable sum of money from a distant relative and decided to use it to run for Congress, against the Republican incumbent.

His campaign manager, at their initial strategy session, was somewhat baffled by the candidate's great reluctance to plan an advertising campaign.

Finally, he asked the man just what he had against advertising.

The would-be Congressman replied: "I tried advertising once in connection with my store. It was a disaster. People came from as far away as the next county. They bought damn near everything I had, and almost put me out of business."

FUND RAISING

One candidate, disgusted after the failure of a 10-dollar-a-plate fundraising dinner, said of his Finance Chairman: "The guy couldn't sell pickles in a maternity ward."

DRUM

After a hard-fought and bitter campaign, a young Republican won a Congressional seat in the November election. His opponent took the loss hard and broke into profanity when the two met about a week after the election.

The new Congressman-elect decided to move his family to Washington early in December to help them adjust to the Capital and to learn his way around before taking office in January. He was surprised when a huge Christmas package arrived for his young son—from the man he had beaten.

But a few days before Christmas, the new Congressman-elect read a slogan on a prominent music store near Capitol Hill, and guessed correctly what the present was.

The slogan read: "If thine enemy wrong thee, buy each of his children a drum."

KENTUCKY COLONEL

In a crowded, stuffy room just off the House floor at the State Capitol, the controversial hearing had been under way for several hours.

The issue involved livestock registration controls, and tempers were growing shorter by the minute.

Into the witness chair stepped a courtly old gentleman with a neatly trimmed white mustache and goatee. An auctioneer by trade, he looked for all the world like the living embodiment of a Kentucky colonel. Over the years he had, in fact, acquired the affectionate title of "Colonel."

A brash young lawmaker knew this and decided to use it to discredit the old man's testimony.

"Tell me, Colonel," he sneered. "Were you a Colonel in the first World War or the second?"

The elderly witness smiled softly. "Well, son," he explained, "I guess the 'Colonel' in front of my name is just like the 'Honorable' in front of yours. It doesn't mean a damn thing."

NAME CARD

At a mammoth political rally, a battery of girls busied themselves at the entrance to the ballroom providing each arriving delegate and speaker with individualized name-cards to be worn throughout the program. Later in the evening, one observant committee member spotted Secretary of Commerce Rogers C. B. Morton without his identity card and was quite miffed. "Where is your name-card?" he inquired. To which Secretary Morton quipped: "Young man, I don't need it anymore—I memorized it!"

CABINET HIGHJINKS

During a break at a recent Cabinet meeting, Secretary of Commerce Rogers C. B. Morton scribbled a note to Secretary Kissinger, seated nearby. It read: "Dear Henry: Today's mail brought a complaining letter from Lawrence of Arabia. He wants to know when you are going to give him back his franchise?"

James E. Akins
U. S. Ambassador to Saudi Arabia

PROHIBITION

"In 1953, prohibition was suddenly slapped on the Kingdom of Saudi Arabia. Saudi citizens had always been forbidden the use of alcohol but foreigners had full access to whatever they wanted. The new prohibition affected all foreigners—even oilmen and (horrors) even diplomats. Our Ambassador at that time was George Wadsworth, an excellent officer and a renowned *bon vivante*. After about six months, Ambassador Wadsworth approached Prince Faisal (who later became King) at a reception, put his arm around the Prince's shoulder and said, 'Your Royal Highness, I understand the reasons for imposing prohibition in the country and I'm not objecting. But it is rather unusual to apply this to diplomats, isn't it? I'm used to having my martini before dinner, wine with my meals and I always like a cognac before I go to bed. My liquor stocks are running very low.' He then smiled broadly and said, 'I'm sure something can be done about it, can't it?' Prince Faisal looked at the Ambassador, smiled equally sweetly and said, 'Of course, Excellency, and we shall miss you.' "

Mark Evans Austad
U. S. Ambassador to Finland

225,000 LETTERS

The largest printing plant of the world is the Rubin H. Donnelly Company. They print magazines like TIME, LIFE and many other important publications and periodicals. They have one fantastic machine that notifies people when their renewal subscriptions are due. One screw lost its tension in this gigantic machine that covers many, many square feet. They would never have known about this mishap if a sheepherder out in Wind River, Wyoming, hadn't received 225,000 letters for him to renew his magazine subscription. The old boy walked ten miles, sent his $6.00 with the following telegram: "Don't send any more. I give up."

SMALL TOWN

The definition of a small town is one where the Velveeta Cheese is in the gourmet section.

KIND WORDS

A busy waitress in a diner received a request from a customer asking for scrambled eggs, bacon, toast and a few kind words. In a few minutes he received the eggs, the bacon and the toast. The customer called back and wanted to know about the kind words. She thought for a few minutes and said, "Don't eat them eggs."

TEXAS OUTHOUSE

A Texan and a New Yorker were arguing about their states. The New Yorker bragged about the World Trade Center stating they

49

didn't have anything like that in Texas. The Texan said, "We have outhouses that big." The New Yorker responded, "You need them."

BED FELLOWS

Politicians make strange bed fellows. The reason is they get used to the same bunk.

MAN OF CALIBER

A man was thinking of retiring from the circus. He decided to quit, he was getting old and was becoming more fearful of being shot out of the cannon. The owner responded that he could not quit, that he would never get another man of his caliber.

SNEAKING SUSPICIONS

A wise philosopher observed in a sneaking suspicion that what is wrong with the world is too damn many sneaking suspicions.

CRYING

Some years ago when John D. Rockefeller died, an old tramp started to cry as he read the headlines. A bystander said, "Why are you crying? John D. Rockefeller was no relative of yours." Whereupon the old tramp stated, "That's what I'm crying about."

NO CONDITION TO TRAVEL

Two youngsters, two boys, grew up learning to hate one another. They argued and fought over girls, marbles, schools and anything else. After they grew up, one became an admiral and the other became an archbishop. At a chance meeting the hatred revived. Both were dressed in their full uniforms. The bishop who was a bit faster, turned to his old adversary and said, "Station Master, which way to Birmingham?" The admiral, not to be outdone, said, "That way, Madam, but are you really in any condition to travel?"

NOAH'S ARK

I liked the stories of Bishop Sheehan. He once said a heckler asked him how many animals there were in the Ark. Bishop Sheehan, in his own wonderful way, said he would ask Noah when he got to Heaven. The heckler replied, "What if he isn't there?" Where upon Bishop Sheehan answered, "You ask him."

John Sherman Cooper
U. S. Ambassador to the German Democratic Republic

PRESS LIGHTLY

In my first campaign for the Senate in 1946, I was shaking hands in front of the Court House in Richmond, Kentucky. Around a Confederate statue, a group of men were sitting, and all shook hands with me, except one who was reluctant to do so.

I said to him, "My name is Cooper, and I am a candidate for the United States Senate."

He responded, "Yes, and I know you are a Republican and your middle name is Sherman. Press my hand lightly."

POST SCRIPT

I wrote a friend in Kentucky a rather long typewritten letter and added a P.S. A few days later he called saying, "I know your post script must be an important message, and my wife and I have studied it for an hour, but can't read your writing." I had to tell him the P.S. said, "I hope to see you soon."

NERVOUS

A well-known government official entered a room in a Washington hotel and began pacing up and down. When a woman asked him what he was doing there, the government official said: "I am going to deliver a speech."

"Do you usually get very nervous before addressing a large audience?" "Nervous?" he replied. "No, I never get nervous."

"In that case," demanded the lady, "what are you doing in the ladies room?"

MARBLES

At a dinner honoring Governor John Reed as Maine's Man of the Year, former Massachusetts Governor Volpe told the following:

"Seeing all these politicians reminds me of the old story about the young man who wanted to become a politician. He knew that in order to succeed he would have to become a good speaker—so he decided to copy Diogenes, the famous Greek who had learned to speak by filling his mouth with pebbles, only he had to fill his mouth with marbles since he didn't happen to have any pebbles. Each day he spoke with his mouth full of marbles and after each practice session he removed one marble. At the end he figured he was a good enough speaker to be a politician—he'd finally lost all his marbles.

Robert F. Bennett
Governor of Kansas

DRIVER'S SEAT

Vern Miller, former Kansas Attorney General, was the Democrat candidate for Governor in 1974, while Robert F. Bennett was the Republican candidate. Miller was famous for his raids and tirades against drugs, gambling and liquor. He is well known for his raid of an Amtrak train that was serving liquor-by-the-drink (which is illegal in Kansas) while passing through the state. Besides ending that practice, Miller's efforts forced airlines to stop serving liquor-by-the-drink on their planes as they travel the skies above Kansas.

Miller's most famous drug raid was accomplished after he emerged from his hiding place in the trunk of a car. That much publicized incident prompted President Gerald Ford to urge in Wichita, Kansas, on November 2, 1974: "Let's put Bennett in the driver's seat and keep Vern Miller in the trunk."

CONFUSION

"Try not to confuse Republicans with Democrats; both of them are confused enough already."

UNDER OATH

A certain Congressman, well known for his special interest in Belly Dancers and his taste for champagne, once appeared before a judge on a traffic violation and resisting arrest. When asked by the judge, "Are you a good Congressman, a good public servant and a good husband?" he replied, "The very best." Upon returning to his seat his lawyer said, "Wasn't your answer a bit egotistical?" The Congressman said, "What else could I say, after all I was under oath."

Otis R. Bowen
Governor of Indiana

TRUCK DRIVER

A truck driver went to the Driver's License Bureau to renew his license. In the course of the examination for relicensure, the driving examiner gave a theoretical problem to the applicant.

The examiner said, "Now supposing you're driving a big truck. It's loaded with steel. You're going down a steep hill and around a curve. On your right is a steep drop-off and on your left is a big cliff. Driving ahead of you about a quarter of a mile is another truck exactly like yours. In between you and this truck is a Volkswagen. You step on your brakes and they fail. What would you do?"

The applicant scratched his head, thought a moment, and said, "You know, when I drive I have a relief driver. His name is Harry. He is usually asleep above me in the cab. I'd wake up Harry."

The driving examiner said, "What good would that do?"

The applicant said, "Oh, it wouldn't do any good, but Harry has never seen a wreck quite like we're gonna have!"

Mills E. Godwin, Jr.
Governor of Virginia

FARMER

Virginia has always been a state with a close personal affiliation with the land. Even today, agriculture is close behind tourism and industrial manufacturing as a source of income. As a consequence, country humor, the native wit of men and women whose sense of the ridiculous helps them to survive the uncertainties of weather and market, has added its own flavor to the humor of politics.

When a former Commissioner of Agriculture sought particularly unflattering words to describe a somewhat dense acquaintance, he quoted a farm neighbor as saying, "That fellow don't know nothin' and he's got that all mixed up."

LOVE

William M. Tuck, who served in the late forties and early fifties, was perhaps the most colorful Virginia Governor of modern times.

Governor Tuck's picturesque language was illustrated by his comment after over-zealous Capitol Police had arrested a young couple for trespassing on the grass. The Governor had just signed an order drafted by the State Agency responsible for the grounds, prohibiting anyone from lying down on the grass. By the time the newspapers got through, the beleaguered Governor was guilty of persecuting the young and thwarting the pathway of true love. Asked later for his personal reaction, the Governor replied, "I felt like a one-legged man at a tail-kicking contest."

POLITICIAN

There is nothing wrong with a political joke as long as it doesn't get elected.

Jays S. Hammond
Governor of Alaska

ALASKA

Remember how lousy things used to be?
Why, before we had oil, fish cluttered the sea.

Yes, black gold sure outglitters the old "silver horde"
Since we reconstituted the Fish and Game Board

With oil stockholders who seldom think petty
After all, as Commissioner, they got J. Paul Getty.

And remember all of those stupid, dumb clucks?
Who complained we might lose a few million ducks?

(A duck, you'll recall, had web feet and a bill
The last one expired the year of "the spill".)

But the woods are now safe, for we've bountied the bears
and all dangerous game, including varying hares.

You know, years ago one could hardly tell
When he was breathing, for air had no smell!

No wonder smoking was popular then
For, though costly, it satisfied some people's yen

To fill up their chests with a rich aroma
And selfishly grow their own carcinoma.

Now everyone has the chance to soak
his lung tissues with hydrocarbonous smoke.

The water drunk then was new and untried
It's a wonder that only a few people died.

True, now that we've grown so much more chummy,
We find that our water may be a bit gummy.

But you know doggone well when you slake your thirst
That the guy survived who drank it first!

Way back then we used to have garbage dumps
Where refuse was piled in unsightly humps.

We've flattened these out now and you can discern
Nice level garbage wherever you turn.

They say God died in those days, and that's on the level.
Can't blame Him anymore for "acts of the devil".

Still, occasionally yet we are brought to our knees
By the sonic boom of the S.S.T.s!

POLLS

As you know, one major expense for politicians these days is the cost of taking polls. It used to be that politicians took their own polls.

There was, for example, the congressional candidate who took some soundings in a rural area. He approached a farmhouse where the farmer's wife was doing the family wash on the front porch.

"I'm Joe Smith running for Congress," he began. "I wonder if I can expect your support?"

At this point, the woman doused him with the wash water, threatened him with a hatchet, shouted that *nobody* named Smith would ever get support from *her* family, and then turned the dogs loose on him.

The candidate retreated a mile or so down the road, took out a pencil and a list of voters in the township, and after the name of the woman wrote: "Doubtful".

FISH

President Hoover's "Fisherman's Prayer" was framed and hung in his suite at the Waldorf Towers:

> God grant that I may fish
> Until my dying day!
> And when it comes to my last cast
> I humbly pray,
> When in God's landing net
> I'm peacefully asleep,
> That in his mercy I be judged
> As good enough to keep.

Arch A. Moore, Jr.
Governor of West Virginia

MOVE FAST

I have earned the reputation of being someone on the move. Because of the rigors of my schedule, it was difficult for those people covering my campaign to maintain the pace as I went from one corner of the state to another. I was constantly being asked to slow down so that they could keep up with me. One harried individual finally pleaded, "For goodness sake, Governor, can't you slow down a bit?" I turned around and looked at him for a moment and said, "You have to realize that a Republican in West Virginia, so outnumbered by Democrats, has to move fast so they won't be able to get a bead on him."

ROAD DIRECTIONS

Another classic I was fond of telling concerns a city slicker in West Virginia for the first time. Before we started building our Interstate highways, West Virginia roads had a deserved national reputation as being tortuous at best. The weary traveler had taken a wrong turn and had gotten lost. Hot and befuddled, he pulled over to a small country store beside a dusty road and asked an elderly mountaineer sitting at the front of the store how to get to his destination.

"Well, let me see," the old man said in a slow West Virginia drawl. "Ya go south along this here road for 'bout a mile 'til ya come up to a fork in the road, an' then ya turn left; go down that there road for about . . . well, no I don't rightly think that's the way ya should go."

Continuing, he said, "Ya better go north up this road just a piece, and then make a right; go for 'bout a mile 'til ya come to a crossroads, and then go west 'til . . . no, that won't work either."

Then the grizzled old man got a gleam in his eye, and standing up he pointed to a road that veered off near the store. "Go down that road through the first intersection to a highway, and then ya turn . . . let's see, which way would ya turn?"

Finally, the mountaineer sat down, took off his hat, wiped the sweat off his forehead with a bright red bandanna, scratched the back of his head and put his hat back on. He looked the traveler squarely in the eye who by this time had a confused and woebegone countenance. After a short pause and then shaking his head, the old man said, "Ya know mister, I don't rightly think that ya can get to that place from here."

Robert D. Ray
Governor of Iowa

IMPRESSION

I recall a young boy who visited my office. The boy walked up to me and said, "I met you before, when you came to my town. I was the one carrying the American flag and you stepped on my foot—you certainly made an impression on me.

INTRODUCTION

After being introduced to speak, I occasionally tell about another time when I was introduced. The man told the audience that it was the first time he had ever introduced a Governor and that he had spent much time thinking of what to say. He wrote for a biography and later called one of my assistants for some suggested remarks. My assistant told him that I preferred a simple, brief introduction. When it was time for him to introduce me, the man told the audience, "I would have given you a long introduction, but I called Governor Ray's office, and they told me that the less said about the Governor, the better."

David F. Cargo
Former Governor of New Mexico

THE WORD

In speaking to various gatherings, I often like to use the following alleged incident in a naval battle of historical fame.

As the *Bon Homme Richard* and the *Serapis* engaged in battle in the War of 1812, they proceeded to fire broadsides furiously at each other. As the battle progressed, the ships came together and were locked with grappling hooks. Opposing seamen swarmed aboard each ship and proceeded into hand-to-hand combat. The blood and sweat were flowing freely. The British captain, feeling that he had the better of it, stood on the bridge of his ship and with megaphone to his mouth, shouted "Do you strike your colors, Sir?" John Paul Jones, the American captain, also by megaphone replied, "Sir, I have not yet begun to fight." And with this one weary American seaman, wiping the blood and sweat from his face looked up and sighed, "There's always some guy don't get the word!"

Ladies and gentlemen, knowing of your interest in our Nation's affairs, I am here to give you "the word."

1984

"Isn't that a disturbing slogan you see every now and then: Peace by 1984—with or without people."

SOBER REAPPRAISAL

"The way those politicians keep calling for a sober reappraisal of the facts—makes you wonder what condition they're in the rest of the time."

BAD BILLS

"Somebody oughta tell the FBI how many bad bills our Senators are passing."

HUBERT HUMPHREY

"I don't want to complain about my mother-in-law but last week she won a Hubert Humphrey look-alike contest."

SHIRLEY TEMPLE

"I used to be a Shirley Temple fan. I can remember her when she was a perfect 36—12-12 and 12 . . ."

MALAPROPS

Twenty years at the Capitol have produced many fine laughs. Here are a few of them as they appeared. Apologies to my good friends in government who are quoted.

Sheriff Clem Michalski—"Milwaukee is the golden egg that the rest of the state wants to milk."

Assemblyman John Pritchard—"If we wait any longer, it will be too late to lock the barn after the horse is stolen."

Senator Gerald D. Lorge—"That was a low blow between the belt."

Senator Casimir Kendziorski—"Why my barber never even graduated from the 4th grade—but he sure learned how to shave while he was there."

Senator Norman Sussman—"The bankers' pockets are bulging with the sweat of the honest working men."

Senator William Trinke—"That's a horse of a different feather."

Ronald Reagan
Former Governor of California

AUTOGRAPH

One day in New York City, I was hurrying down 5th Avenue on my way back to the hotel when about 30 feet in front of me a man stopped suddenly, pointed his finger at me and in a loud voice said, "Ah hah! I know you. I see you all the time in the 'pitchas' and on the T.V." He came at me while he was talking, fumbling in his pockets for pen and paper. All the time he kept up his loud declaration that he knew me and had seen me in the movies and on T.V.

Everyone on the street had stopped and was watching as he approached. When he finally got to me he thrust the pen and paper at me triumphantly and said, "I gotta have your autograph, Ray Milland!" So I signed Ray Milland—there was no point in disappointing him.

FOREIGN AID

A few years ago, I had the privilege of representing our country on a mission that involved meeting with the heads of state of several European countries. Because of the nature of the mission, I'd been encouraged to take the family but Ron was the only one of the children who could make the trip with Nancy and myself.

After a steady schedule of rather formal state dinners and receptions, we found ourselves in Paris with a free night. The three of us decided to have dinner at the world famous Maxim's. Now the usual procedure is that security men take a table somewhat removed from ours and they also handle the matter of paying the check, etc.—billing us later. Because of this, I very seldom have much money with me. On this night I had a single $5 dollar bill in my pocket. Then the unforeseen happened. Down between the tables, in our direction, came a strolling violinist. Maybe I hadn't caught up with inflation but I figured if he stopped at our table, one dollar was about right—certainly not $5.

Quickly, I asked Nancy if she had any money. The answer was no. "Ron?", I said desperately, and got an incredulous "are you kidding?". The violinist was almost upon us. "Don't anyone look up", I said. We began concentrating on our salad. He stopped right beside us and started playing, "California, Here I Come". I just handed him the $5 and wrote it off as foreign aid.

SECURITY

There was another incident involving security back in 1968 when there was so much rioting and disturbance in the country.

It was late at night. Nancy and I were awakened by the unmistakable sound of a shot. I went downstairs and learned that two men had been seen lighting the fuse of a molotov cocktail with the evident intention of fire bombing the house. The guard got off one shot but they made their getaway in a car.

Now everywhere in the world a molotov cocktail is a coke bottle (or it's counterpart) filled with gasoline—not in California. Ours was a magnum size champagne bottle—California champagne.

I was the speaker at a banquet in one of our central valley towns several years ago. Security around the building by the local police and sheriff's deputies was unusually heavy because of demonstrations by the "Welfare Rights Organization", protesting our welfare reforms which, incidentally, resulted in a 43% grant increase to the truly deserving needy.

One man persistently questioned the officers and others as to which door I'd use in leaving the building. Then he turned up repeatedly circling the block in his car. The police decided to stop him on his next time around but he disappeared before they could do this. Thoroughly aroused and suspicious, an "all points bulletin" went out but, in the meantime, he returned, slowly circling the block again. On his second round they flagged him down and hustled him out of the car.

He seemed to understand what the trouble was. "No! No!", he protested, "you've got me all wrong! I just want to see the son of a ----!"

OLDEST PROFESSION

"You know, politics has been called the second oldest profession," he says. "Sometimes there is a similarity to the first."

ADAM AND EVE

"I sometimes think Adam and Eve were Russians. They didn't have a roof over their head, nothing to wear, but they had one apple between them and they thought that was Paradise."

MOUSETRAP

"I always grew up believing that if you build a better mousetrap, the world will beat a path to your door. Now if you build a better mousetrap the government comes along with a better mouse."

RECEPTIONIST

When I chose a receptionist in my first Congressional office in 1969, I explained that anyone entering my office must be preceded with a card bearing the name of the individual—NO EXCEPTIONS, NOT EVEN MY MOTHER.

One month later a card appeared—THIS IS YOUR MOTHER AND STEPFATHER, MR. & MRS. AMON BUTLER.

Bill Brock
U. S. Senator, Tennessee

THE GOOSE ISSUE

A candidate for constable in a small Tennessee town was trying to meet the issue of whether people should be allowed to let their geese run at large or keep them penned.

The first visit was to a house which had a nice lawn and flowers, and the candidate, thinking this was a place where the occupants would favor keeping the geese penned up, responded to the question of whether he was for or against the issue. He said he was for keeping the geese penned up. The lady slammed the door in his face, advising at the same time he would not have her support.

The next house had a barren yard, and here, he thought the occupants would be for letting geese run at large. "How do you stand on the question of keeping geese penned or allowed to run at large?" was posed by the lady who came to the door. Immediately, he said he was for permitting them to run at large. The door was slammed in his face with a pledge of non-support.

At the third house, when the lady responded to his knock, he immediately said, "I am John Jones, running for constable, and I want to tell you right now that I am all right on this goose question."

VOTE RIGHT

I think one of my favorite stories is the one told by Ronald Reagan when he was campaigning for governor. He had just finished making a speech and a man came up to him with the following:

"Mr. Reagan, they told me during the last presidential campaign that if I voted Republican, the United States would be in war in less than six months. I voted the Republican ticket and sure enough the United States was in war in less than six months."

SIN

One of my favorite anecdotes that I have used many times in talking with groups in explaining how much easier it is to talk about cutting government expenses, than to do it:

A ministerial student thought that if he was going to preach about sin, he needed to find out something about it. He went to a cocktail lounge and before he knew it he had had too many cocktails. He started for home and fell on a sidewalk that had just been poured with the cement still wet. He passed out and the next morning they had to chisel him out of the sidewalk. When he got back to the dormitory, the boys asked him what he had found out on his experiment. He said, "Well, fellows, this sin business may be just fine in the abstract, but it's sure hell in the concrete."

Carl T. Curtis
U. S. Senator, Nebraska

MUSIC

My mother wanted me to become an opera singer. The family did not have much money, but they secured the best voice teacher possible and I started out to reach this goal.

At my first public appearance, I was to sing "Carry Me Back to Old Virginia." It was to be a solo. As I started to sing, a lady in the front row started to cry. As I continued with the words of "Carry Me Back to Old Virginia," tears just rolled down her cheeks. When I finished, she was sobbing.

In a few minutes, I went over to this lady and I said, "I take it you are from Virginia." Her reply was, "No, I'm a musician."

Thereupon I gave up my career in music and decided to enter politics.

CAREER

"What plans have you made for your son?" the preacher's friend asked.

"I've always believed that a child should map his own future," replied the minister, "so I conducted a little test the other day. I put an apple, a Bible and a silver dollar in a room and suggested that he go in there and play. The theory was that if we found him playing with the Bible I would devote my time in teaching him the ministry. If we discovered that the apple attracted his attention he would probably like to become an agriculturist. And if we found him playing with the silver dollar we figured that he would grow up to become a banker."

71

"And which of the three did he choose?" asked the friend.

"When we went into the room," the preacher explained, "we found him sitting on the Bible, eating the apple from his right hand and clutching the silver dollar with his left hand. We were forced to admit then that he probably would grow up to be a politician."

Bob Dole
U. S. Senator, Kansas

COW STEALING

In 1971, I introduced a resolution to repeal the Gulf of Tonkin Resolution, which had become the scapegoat for our Vietnam involvement and the repeal of which had taken on the aspects of a political football which had little to do with the real substance of the Vietnam debate.

Senator J. William Fulbright, who also had the repeal idea, took some offense at my action and accused me of having "stolen" his amendment.

"Stealing a man's amendment is like stealing his cow," Fulbright complained.

But I reminded him that it was National Dairy Week and I would never steal a man's cow during National Dairy Week.

"I just milked it a little," I admitted.

MEMORY TAX

I walked into the Senate chamber one day and Senator Humphrey was talking. An hour later he was still talking.

During his speech, Senator Humphrey remarked, "now gentlemen, let me tax your memories."

Just then, Senator McGovern jumped up and shouted, "why haven't we thought of that before?"

NIGHTMARE

My hometown newspaper, the *Russell Record*, once reported on a conscientious Congressman who kept having a recurrent nightmare

73

in which he dreams that all the money he is spending is his own.

LONG WINDED

The Senate floor discussion had gone on for a long time and the hour was growing late, as Senator Hartke settled in for what looked like it was going to be a lengthy contribution to the debate.

Following Senate procedure, I interrupted politely by asking if the Senator would yield for a question.

Generously, Senator Hartke indicated that he would be glad to yield for a question.

"Does the Senator intend to speak for long?" I inquired.

Hartke indicated that he did have a great deal to say on the subject.

Will there be time enough for me to go to my office and return before the Senator is finished, I went on.

Senator Hartke allowed as how he thought there might be enough time for that.

"My Kansas office?" I replied.

74

Pete V. Domenici
U. S. Senator, New Mexico

PUT DOWN

When I was first elected, I thought being a Senator made me the greatest thing in the world. It took one of my twin girls to restore my perspective.

One day I decided to stay home late so I could spend some time with the twins, who often didn't see me except when the other six children were also at home. As the twins played on the floor, totally ignoring my presence, I began to get irritated. After all, I thought, I stayed home for them and I am a Senator and they should be happy to spend time with me.

I clapped my hands to get their attention. They continued to ignore me. I clapped a second time, more loudly, and Paula turned around, fixed me with a stare, and said firmly, "Daddy, you is no king, you is just a Senator." I left for the office soon after.

WRONG DECISION

I won't forget what I heard a man say at one of the earliest political events I ever attended.

He had suffered a long harangue from hecklers in the crowd, who believed that democracy wouldn't work because it took so long.

"Democracy may be slow and sometimes it seems to stumble to the right decision, but that's better than going full-speed ahead to the wrong decision."

ITALIAN REPRESENTATION

Early in my Senatorial career I was invited to a meeting of Republican Italians in the Northeast. Now, where I'm from you can hold a meeting of Republican Italians in the corner drugstore with room left over, so I told my wife, Nancy, not to expect much of a crowd.

Well, I was flabergasted to find more than 1,000 people at this event. I made what I thought was a good speech and they applauded and I thought the evening was about over. But, on the way to my seat, a man stood up near the front of the crowd and asked, "Senator, how many Italians do you have on your staff?"

I thought I had misunderstood him, so I asked him to repeat his question.

He did, in a more aggressive voice.

"Well, mister," I said with a smile, "with the small number of Italians in my state, they are substantially over-represented with just me in the office."

Paul J. Fannin
U. S. Senator, Arizona

SORRY

I was on the plane going from Washington to Chicago and the stewardess, who was a former Arizonan, recognized me and came over and said, "Are you still Governor of Arizona?" I replied, "No, I am the U.S. Senator," and she said, "Oh, I am sorry."

TWO MORE QUESTIONS

While I was governor my son, a recent graduate from law school, awaiting the bar exams, worked in my office without pay. After taking the bar exams he was working in a downtown law office, so I still sought his legal advice. On my second trip to his office to seek advice I noticed a sign on his desk: "Three Questions Answered $50." I said, "Bobby, what does that mean?" He said, "Dad, you have two more questions."

TELL YOUR SIDE

At a social function I was introduced to a young lady who said, "I have heard so much about you—now I would like to give you a chance to tell your side."

Ph.D

A Ph.D was trying to put together a toy he had ordered for his son's birthday. After reading the instructions and trying in vain for 30 minutes, he gave up, put all the parts back in the box and took it outside where a man was mowing the lawn.

"Could you put this together?" the Ph.D asked of his caretaker.

The caretaker pulled the parts out of the box and quickly assembled the toy.

"You did that without even looking at the instructions," the amazed Ph.D said.

"When you can't read," replied the caretaker, "you have to use your head."

Jake Garn
U. S. Senator, Utah

SAINT PETER

A politician and a priest arrived at the pearly gates at the same time. Both knocked at the gate. Saint Peter peered out, immediately threw open the gates, proclaiming "He's here! He's here!" and rushed to the politician, as trumpets began to sound, flutes began to play, and a chorus of angels sang a celestial greeting.

In the rush and excitement, the priest was knocked down. As he struggled to his feet and began to follow after the happy throng, the pearly gates slammed shut in his face. Shaken and confused, he knocked again. Saint Peter looked out, opened the gates, and let the priest enter.

"I don't understand it, Saint Peter," the priest began. "I have served God all my life, dedicated myself to the salvation of mankind, and I arrive at the pearly gates and am completely ignored—literally downtrodden—in the midst of the tremendous welcome for, of all people, a POLITICIAN! I just don't understand!"

"Oh, Father, I am so sorry!" explained Saint Peter. "But, you see, we get a great many priests entering through the pearly gates, but this is the first politician we've ever had!"

DECIDING VOTE

Addressing a group in the southern part of Utah, then-Mayor Jake Garn began by saying that just before he had left, the five-man Salt Lake City Commission passed a resolution wishing him Godspeed and a safe return. He was very appreciative of the fact, except that the resolution passed three to two. He had to cast the deciding vote.

79

ANYBODY UP THERE?

The mayor of a large western city had just about the worst day possible for an elected official. Everything seemed to be going wrong. He finally just stormed out of his office, telling his secretary that he was going for a walk.

Not far from City Hall was a lane leading along the edge of a precipice with a beautiful view of the valley and the mountains beyond. The Mayor walked along the lane, breathing in the fresh air and taking in the magnificent view. He was just to the point of saying that life was really not that bad, after all, when the earth beneath him gave way, and he toppled over the edge of the precipice.

As he fell, he grabbed a branch growing out from the side of the cliff face and hung there for a few moments, catching his breath. As he considered his position, with no apparent way to get safely up or down, it occurred to him to ask for help. He looked skyward and yelled "Is anybody up there?" There was no reply. Again: "Is anybody up there?!"

A deep voice responded, "Yes, my son. I am here."

"Oh, Lord, please help me! I'll do anything you ask."

"I will help you," said the Lord, "but first you must have faith."

"Oh, Lord, I have faith. I have FAITH!" replied the Mayor.

"Then, let go of the branch," said the Lord.

The Mayor hung for a moment longer, pondering the situation, and then yelled, "Is anybody else up there?"

80

THE CANDIDATE

Mr. Vice President, Mr. Chairman, My Favorite Congressman, Friends and Fellow Members of the Alfalfa Party: You are to be congratulated. You have made the perfect selection. I am the ideal candidate. I have had experience. I have had an audience with the Pope. I have talked with Golda Meier. I have visited the Wailing Wall. I have been to Vietnam. The New York Times Encyclopedia has me listed as a Democrat. The Senate Clerk calls me a Republican. Bill Buckley's National Review calls me a Conservative. And the Washington Post calls me a Neanderthal.

EXTREMISM

After all, extremism in the pursuit of votes is no vice, and moderation in the pursuit of money is no virtue.

I have been called an extremist. That's not quite true. I only go to extremes when I'm arranging my own defeat.

SELF-MADE MEN

There's one thing about the Democratic candidates—all of them are self-made men—and this takes a load off The Almighty—saves him a lot of embarrassment.

TWO PARTY SYSTEM

My friend, Jim Buckley, tells me that the way to preserve a two-party system is to win election on a third-party ticket.

SEX

You know, sex is a lot like politics. You don't have to be good at it to enjoy it. People have asked me what I think of sex in the streets. Well, it may be one of the newer ways to demonstrate against the establishment, but it's got to be damned uncomfortable.

CONSERVATISM

Now, on the subject of "Speed," I am entirely clear. Like any good Conservative, I am against it. This country has been moving too fast for too long a time. In fact, I have been known—in my moments of arch Conservatism—to yell: "Stop the world; I want to get off."

MARRIAGE

I wish my son could be here tonight but as some of you know, he's on his honeymoon. I sure hope that marriage works out. She's a liberal, and he's a conservative and *it's murder for a guy who's wife is always wrong.*

TELEPHONE

We kid about the President but it's not an easy job. Just look at all the leaks in this administration. The other day I telephoned the White House, got the Oval Room on the President's private line, told one of my best jokes and the only one who laughed was Jack Anderson.

PRAYER

I don't know whether to believe Teddy when he says he's not running for the nomination. I heard the other day that he called *DIAL-A-PRAYER* and asked if there were any messages.

POLITICAL FAVORS

John Sharp Williams, one of Mississippi's famous post Civil War Senators, told an aide one day that an incident had amazed him so much that it would take him some time to recover. Asked for an explanation, he was quoted to this effect:

"I've helped John Doe, sheriff of Cocahoma County, on quite a few occasions. I have just learned that he did a favor for me. It is the only instance I can recall in which a person I helped didn't hold it against me."

FARMER

An Arkansas politician was scrounging for votes in a close election. Although it was autumn, it was so hot that the candidate hired an air-conditioned car, a rarity at the time, in which to campaign. On a gravel road in a rural section, he happened to spy a man he was looking for, a tight-fisted, but influential farmer, trudging towards the nearest town. Since the sun was beating down, the politician stopped the car, found out where the pedestrian was going and offered him a ride. The latter accepted and, after the usual small talk, the candidate began his sales talk. He was upset when the farmer suddenly asked that the car be stopped, saying he wanted to get out. The office-seeker asked what he had done to offend him, if anything. "No offense," his passenger replied, "but it's turned so cold so quick that I got to hurry back home and kill hogs."

THE COMMON MAN

Theodore G. Bilbo, Mississippi rabble-rouser and one-time

Senator, used to tell this one to illustrate his affection for the common man.

One of his mentors, he said, was a Mississippi politician called "Private" John Allen because he made much of his foot soldier status during the Civil War. One of his opponents in a race for Congress was a former General in the Confederate Army. During a joint debate, the former high-ranking officer made much of his standing and exploits during the War. Allen replied that he too had been in the Confederate Army, but served in the ranks. He had many hardships and confessed, that on one or two hot occasions, he ran but did quite a bit of fighting too. He continued that since they both fought for the Lost Cause they should be able to reach a sensible and amicable agreement about the veteran's vote.

"Let all the former generals vote for my opponent," he proposed, "and let all the state's veterans who were privates vote for me."

Then, tossing back his head, Bilbo would shout:

"Let all the rich men vote for my opponent for he loves them. Let all the poor men—and God knows I love them—vote for me."

Paul Laxalt
U. S. Senator, Nevada

FRESH AIR

A man from Los Angeles visited the scenic Lake Tahoe area in western Nevada. Upon returning to Los Angeles, he was asked by a friend how he enjoyed his visit to Lake Tahoe. The man replied that he found the country beautiful but the entire three days he was there he was frightened to death, actually terrified.

"Why," asked his friend.

"Just imagine I had to breathe air for three days that I couldn't even see," replied the Los Angeles man.

INSTANT DEFLATION

At times politics can be a real "downer."

For thirteen long months I was involved in a spirited contest for the Governorship of Nevada with the incumbent, Grant Sawyer.

After our successful election when I was on the usual "Head Trip", I decided to tour the high schools of the state. Each succeeding visit I was more warmly greeted and my ego under went a bit of the usual inflating.

My tour of the schools took me to a small rural high school in Western Nevada where the Student Body President nervously introduced me to his classmates. He read carefully from prepared note cards and was proceeding rather well. Then, laying the cards on the rostrum, he looked up at his fellow students and proclaimed, "And now I have the honor and pleasure to introduce to you Governor Grant Sawyer!"

WOW—talk about instant deflation!

DEMOCRAT

Politician—"And in conclusion, my friends, I wish to state that I was born a Democrat, always have been a Democrat, and expect to die a Democrat."

Heckler—"Not very ambitious, are you?"

Charles McC. Mathias, Jr.
U. S. Senator, Maryland

ANGELS

As a freshman in the House I was joined outside the restaurant in the Capitol by a very senior colleague from the deep, deep South. His guests arrived before mine and they were a truly challenging spectacle to a young man who had led a protected life in the hills of rural Maryland. They were all ladies of a certain age; loud, generally overweight and universally disheveled by a morning's sightseeing in the heat and humidity of a Washington summer.

At that moment I learned the true meaning of seniority, because only an experienced professional could have faced such a force, not only with equanimity, but with style and verve.

Without a moments hesitation he threw open his arms in welcome and shouted down the corridor to his bedraggled female consituents, "They must have declared a holiday in heaven to let all you angels out today!"

Bob Packwood
U. S. Senator, Oregon

KITTENS

There's the story about the little kid who is selling kittens. A man walks by and asks the kid if they're Republican or Democratic kittens. The kid says, "They're Democratic kittens." The guy says, "Sorry, I don't want to buy any."

About a week later, the same guy is walking by and the kid is still selling kittens. And he says to the kid, "Are those Republican or Democratic kittens?" the kid says,

"They're Republican kittens." The guy says, "Last week when I went by here, you told me they were Democratic kittens. Now you tell me they're Republican kittens. How did they change?"

The kid says, " 'Cause now they got their eyes open!"

TOASTMASTER

The banqueteers were chatting in little groups of twos and threes and seemed to be having a good time. The toastmaster turned to the first speaker and said, "Shall I let them enjoy themselves a little longer, or shall I introduce you?"

JACK BENNY

The famous comedian, Jack Benny, was invited to visit Harry Truman, and he approached the White House carrying his violin case. A Secret Service man stopped him and said, "What have you got in that case?" And to be funny, he said, "I've got a machine gun." The Secret Service man said, "Thank God! I thought it was your violin!"

Charles H. Percy
U. S. Senator, Illinois

HIGHER OFFICE

All candidates know, to their detriment, that the press always suspects that they're using their current campaign as a stepping stone to higher office. That happened to me in 1964 when I ran for Governor of Illinois. Finally I told my campaign manager to set the record straight once and for all. He faced a full-dress press conference and inadvertently declared: "Chuck Percy is interested in one office and one office only—Governor—of the United States!"

CAMPAIGN SLOGAN

The Democrats loved Barry Goldwater. They got a great deal of pleasure from his campaign slogan, "In your heart you know he's right". They would add, "Yes, extremely right."

POLITICIAN

Advice to a politician: "Always be sincere, whether you mean it or not."

Hugh Scott
U. S. Senator, Pennsylvania

VOS OMNES

I've often been asked who my favorite Senator is. I have to go with Cicero. After all, he was the first Senator to say "y'all" (*vos omnes*).

DEMOCRATS

The Democrats are in pretty good shape. All they need are leaders, issue and money.

49 MINUTE WEEK

We're having a little trouble with the House of Representatives. It appears they're hooked on economizing. They've agreed to a 49-minute work week. In fact, the last time they had a quorum call the operator cut in and said they had reached a non-working number.

REPUBLICANS TRY HARDER

Meanwhile, back in the Senate, we Republicans in Minority are trying harder. Like Avis. Mike and I have an agreement. No matter what he asks for, I give him Arpege. I am not only trying harder, but I am trying as I know how to be. Mike and I have other agreements: he makes his political remarks on Tuesdays and I make mine on Thursdays. On Mondays he praises the Blue Sky Country and on Wednesday I chant the glories of the Keystone State. Anybody wanting to talk about Florida or California climate has to get a unanimous consent.

PISMIRE

In debate, one of my favorite words is "pismire". Everybody thinks it's a dirty word. Actually, it's a little red ant.

OBSTRUCTIONISTS

Reporter: Does the $507 million refugee assistance bill asked by the President have a chance in the House?

"I believe that the present obstructionist House may nitpick and meanly and cheaply cut here and there. I hope whatever is needed should be passed. If this President asked some members of the House to observe Sunday as a holy day, they would vote to change it to Wednesday. There are some maverick obstructionists over there who have a feisty feeling. It isn't all bad . . ."

Reporter: What is this feistiness you're talking about?

"They're feisty against the President and I think that the public eventually will hold them highly irresponsible. I call them the 'nugatories.'" Reporter: You made us all look that one up yesterday, Senator!

Reporter: Well, what about moving holy days from Sunday to Friday or Saturday?

"Well, I'm not going to walk into that one. I avoided saying Friday or Saturday after all my years in politics. Friday is the Moslem holy day. Did you know that I organized everybody but the Druids in my last campaign?"

DIEGO GARCIA

Reporter: What is your prediction on Diego Garcia?

"I have no prediction on Diego Garcia . . . I've always admired his paintings . . . I support the Administration's position but it's being seized on as a larger issue."

Reporter: What about the fact, that I've read, that the island has an altitude of only about three feet? Don't you worry about its being hit by a big wave?

"I would if I lived on it."

Reporter: So, how do you feel about the proposal to spend $180 million on an island only three feet tall?

"I hope a meteorologist has talked to the Navy."

William L. Scott
U. S. Senator, Virginia

POLITICIANS

During a political campaign, a lady indicated that she did not participate in politics or have any use for politicians, and the precinct worker attempted to show the importance of citizen participation in the affairs of government and concluded with the statement, "You do vote, don't you?" To which the lady replied, "No, it only encourages them."

WHO'S THAT

I enjoyed the statement:
"An office holder who loses contact with his constituents soon goes from *Who's Who* to "Who's that'."

Robert T. Stafford
U. S. Senator, Vermont

PERSUASION

Sometimes we Republicans find that we are talking to people who are already of our persuasion and realize we ought to be talking to constituents who are not members of the Republican Party. They are the ones we have to persuade.

This situation reminds me of the clergyman who for a long period of time had attempted to get a young woman of dubious reputation to attend services at his church. He knew she needed to be converted from her wayward practices. Finally, one Sunday she showed up. When services were over, the Reverend said, "I am so delighted that you have finally attended services in my church. I was praying for you all last night." The girl replied, 'Why didn't you call? I would have been over here in 10 minutes."

POLITICAL ADVERTISING

WANTED: Intelligent, handsome, well-educated man with money to run for Congress. Send money to Republican Congressional Campaign Committee, Washington, D.C.

MARTINI

An important Senator and his wife went to a party at the British Embassy. It wasn't long after that the Senator felt it necessary to tell his wife, "Darling, that's the 5th martini you've had in less than 15 minutes. Aren't you embarrassed to go to the bar so often?" "No, why should I be" she gleefully replied, "I just tell the bartender it's for you."

ABSENT-MINDED

A preacher's wife, a physician's wife and a traveling salesman's wife were waiting for the fourth at bridge one day when one of them brought up the subject of forgetfulness.

"I think my husband is the most forgetful man alive," declared the preacher's wife, "because he often forgets his notes and has to stumble through his sermon in a deplorable manner."

"I think my husband is even more forgetful than that," said the physician's wife. "He never can seem to remember to take his medicine bag and has to come all the way home for something he needs."

"My husband," said the traveling salesman's wife, "came home the other day, tipped his hat politely to me and said, 'Haven't I seen you somewhere before?' "

PRESIDENT TAFT

President William Howard Taft was holding a reception one day when his tailor arrived to fit Taft's new Prince Albert. The tailor was hustled into the reception line by zealous guards. When he reached the President, Taft remarked, "You look very familiar to me." "Naturally, Mr. President," chuckled the tailor. "I made your pants." "Ah yes," nodded the President. "How do you do, Major Pants."

ISSUES AND ANSWERS

Before taking questions after a speech, I sometimes caution that I won't always be able to come up with an answer, citing the time

94

that my wife, substituting for me, agreed to take questions. A man in the back of the room asked a question which she interpreted as wanting to know my opinion on current ladies fashions. She replied saying that she knew I was impressed by mini's, that I don't like maxi's, and that I hadn't made up my mind on midi's. The man rose to his feet again and said, "Thank you, Madame, but what I wanted to know was your husband's position on the Mid East."

Strom Thurmond
U. S. Senator, South Carolina

TOWN IDIOT

During my last campaign for re-election I was speaking in a small town in my state. The next day, I was walking along the street with a friend and a young man stopped to speak.

"Isn't this Senator Thurmond?" he asked.

"Yes it is," I responded.

"I heard you speak last night."

"How did you like it?"

"I thought it was the worst speech I have ever heard. It was terrible," he said.

"Well," I said half smiling, "I'll try to do better next time."

My friend who was upset at the young man's frankness tried to console me. "Don't worry about that boy. Nobody pays any attention to him. He's the town idiot. Why, he merely repeats what he's heard others say."

JUROR

Talesman number five was called to the stand. Evidently he had never been in a courtroom before. Looking straight at the man questioning him he said, "I'm afraid I wouldn't make a good juror." "Why not?" he was asked. "Because I've formed my opinion already. As soon as I laid eyes on you I knew you were as guilty as the devil." "Well," replied his redfaced questioner, "Fortunately for me I am not on trial. I am the District Attorney."

96

PRISON SPEECH

While Governor of South Carolina I made a speech to the inmates at the South Carolina prison in Columbia. I unfortunately began with the familiar, "I am happy to be here and I am glad to see you here." You can imagine the reaction I received.

John G. Tower
U. S. Senator, Texas

GEORGE WASHINGTON

When George Washington was very young he and his daddy lived on a big ranch in West Texas. One day George's daddy was called out to the west forty to round up a maverick stray. While his daddy was gone, George went out to play.

Now it happened that between the bunkhouse and the corral there was growing a beautiful mesquite tree. George's daddy loved that tree. Not just because it was a beautiful mesquite tree, but because it was the only tree for thirty miles in any direction. Long after sundown George's daddy returned from the range to find the mesquite tree lying in the dust.

"George," he said, "What happened to my tree?"

"I did it," George said. "I whittled it down with my trusty Bowie knife. I CANNOT TELL A LIE!"

"You'll never get along in Texas, son," his daddy said. "Pack your bedroll, we're moving to Virginia."

SOUTHERN DEMOCRATS

Texas is a predominantly Democratic state and I grew up in a family of Southern Democrats. My grandfather grew up in Texas during the Reconstruction period and had no use for Republicans.

One kinsman of mine once told me, "John, I'm glad your grand-daddy died before you became a Republican—it would have broken his heart."

Shortly after my election in 1961, as the first Republican Senator from Texas since the Reconstruction period, my father remarked. "Son, the family's proud of you and I think most of them even voted for you."

Bill Archer
Congressman, 7th, Texas

TRUTH

Democrat—"I would like to suggest that we dispense with mud-slinging in this campaign."

Republican—"An excellent suggestion, sir. If you will refrain from telling lies about the Republican party, I will give you my assurance that I will withhold the truth about the Democratic party."

SPEECH WRITER

Whenever I get up to deliver a prepared speech before a large group, I'm reminded of the story about a former Senator who had such an excellent speech writer that the Senator never bothered to read his speeches before he delivered them in public. The speech writer was understandably upset one day when the Senator refused him a pay raise and indicated that the young man wasn't worth a dime more than he was being paid and should instead be grateful for the opportunity to work for such a distinguished American. The next day, the Senator arrived, unread prepared speech in hand, at a convention of some 10,000 veterans in the state capital. He took his place at the podium and began to read: "Gentlemen, this state and nation owe you their very existence. It's high time we did something for you in return for your gallant service . . . so today I would like to spell out for you the details of a comprehensive 37 point program I have personally developed to bring this about." The Senator turned to the second page, curious himself about the details of the program . . . but all he saw written there was, "O.K. you S.O.B. You're on your own!"

John M. Ashbrook
Congressman, 17th, Ohio

LONG WINDED

The politician was speaking to the local service clubs and rattled on for an hour and a half before glancing at his watch and remarking ... "They didn't tell me how long I could speak" ... He was interrupted by a voice from the back of the room ... "There's a calendar right behind you."

IDENTITY PROBLEM

I had represented the City of Ashland for six years and was engaged in a campaign for re-election. One brisk October afternoon I was approaching one of Ashland's worst intersections when I saw a rather elderly lady looking around rather helplessly because of the traffic pattern that really was not set up for the benefit of a pedestrian. I helped her across the street and when I was in the middle of the road, I thought to myself that if anyone saw me, they would think I was helping this little old lady just because I was a candidate running for re-election. I did not tell her who I was or use the opportunity to campaign. When we had safely alighted on the other side and I started to leave, she grabbed my arm and said, "Young man, I've been walking across that intersection for years and you're the first person who ever helped me. If I can ever help you, let me know." I thought to myself, "Oh well, she brought it up, I didn't, so I'll do a little electioneering." I smiled rather hesitantly and said, "Well, yes you can help me. I am running for Congress." Just as fast as a flash she said, "I certainly will help you. We have to get rid of that man who is in there now."

Clarence J. Brown, Jr.
Congressman, 7th, Ohio

GOVERNMENT SPENDING

London, Ohio
July 26, 1967

Congressman Clarence J. Brown, Jr.
Washington, D.C.

Dear Sir:

I have a dependent relative who has very little fiscal responsibility. He means well, but he keeps buying presents for my parents and me, charging them to our account!

When he sees something that he thinks we might need, he buys it and we have to pay. These things are rarely what we'd have bought ourselves. Because he doesn't work for a living, money doesn't mean much to him. He is generous to the poor and needy with my money and gives to the unworthy, too.

We just received a bill for his last spending spree, and it gives me a sick, hopeless feeling. How much better things would be if we could spend our own money for the things we want!

He won't listen to me, but he will listen to you. Please, please use your influence to cut the spending of my Uncle Sam.

Truly yours,
Reimund Manneck

While I cannot vouch for the originality of this problem. I see in it a statement reflecting the situation and concern of millions of American citizens.

William S. Cohen
Congressman, 2nd, Maine

PUBLIC ETHICS

After Henry Ford had made a fortune in the automobile industry, he decided to return to the land his father had emigrated from, County Cork, Ireland. Ford's fame had gone before him and upon arrival in Cork he was greeted by a committee of public-minded citizens who were trying to raise money for a new hospital. Ford immediately took out his checkbook and wrote a check for $5,000. The next day in the newspaper there appeared a full page ad thanking Mr. Ford for his generous contribution of $50,000 which would allow the community to complete its hospital. Later in the day, the Committee reappeared at Ford's door apologizing profusely stating that error was the type-setter's fault and that they would certainly print a retraction in the following day's paper. Ford considered this option for a minute and said—"I think I have a better idea." He told the Committee he would make out a check for the additional $45,000 if they would allow him to have something inscribed over the main entrance. That was an offer the Committee couldn't refuse. Consequently, Ford made out the check and chose a scripture from Matthew which can be seen today, "I came among you as a stranger and you took me in."

James M. Collins
Congressman, 3rd, Texas

FUND RAISING

Republican Women—There was a big explosion at a Women's Club, killing them all. St. Peter met them at the Pearly Gates and said, "Ladies, there has been a mix-up in the bookkeeping and we don't have room for you right now. We will have to send you down to the other place till we find room for you here in heaven. Please be patient, it won't be long." A couple of weeks went by, and St. Peter got a frantic telephone call from Satan, asking him to please take the women back. St. Peter said, "I can't. I've got trouble finding room for them." Satan said, "You've got troubles! You don't know what these women are doing! With their cake bakes, garage sales and bazaars, they've almost got enough money to air-condition this place!"

EXECUTIVE

A good executive is a man who will share the credit with the man who did all the work.

POLITICS

I have been in politics now for five terms. It is an interesting life. I take it in stride. I sleep just like a baby. I go to bed and I sleep an hour, and I wake up bawling and cry for two hours.

Silvio O. Conte
Congressman, 1st, Massachusetts

NUTTY LEGISLATION

DURING GENERAL DEBATE ON H.R. 4296, EMERGENCY FARM PRICE SUPPORT BILL, ON THE FLOOR OF THE HOUSE, MARCH 19, 1975.

Mr. Chairman: I rise to inform members of an amendment I will offer to this bill. My amendment is entirely consistent with its principles and goals.

My opinion of H.R. 4296 is this: "Nuts!"

The title of my new program is: "Subsidies for nuts."

Of course, I realize that any target price or loan level will seem like an arbitrary figure. But, as H.R. 4296 has shown, all target price and loan levels are wholly imaginary figures. They have lost all relationship to the cost of production, even though that's required by the 1973 Agriculture Act.

Since farm loans offer the only lending program in which the lendee, not the lendor, profits, I have added a special provision for the Congress.

I have noted that on the West Lawn of the Capitol, there are several historic chestnut trees. For the products of these trees, Congress could set a special target price and loan level. I would suggest a loan level of one thousand dollars a pound, which seems sufficiently unrelated to the cost of production to fit in with this bill. For the thousand pound harvest anticipated this autumn, the Congress could apply for a million dollar non-recourse loan from the federal treasury, putting up nuts for collateral.

Then, next October, if the market price for Capitol chestnuts hasn't reached the one thousand dollars a pound level, the Congress can default on the loan, keep the million bucks, send the nuts to Butz, and waltz merrily to the bank without paying any penalty or interest.

But I wouldn't let my nutsy program rip off the consumer. I would rebate the million dollars from this nutty loan to the tax-payers, to repay them for the time and expense the House has wasted on this terrible piece of legislation.

TEXT OF THE AMENDMENT TO H.R. 4296 OFFERED BY MR. CONTE: Page 2, after line 25, add this new section:

"(c) NOT WITHSTANDING THE PROVISIONS OF SECTION 301 OF THIS ACT OR COMMON SENSE, THE SECRETARY SHALL MAKE AVAILABLE TO PRODUCERS LOANS AND PUR-CHASES ON THE 1975 CROP OF FRUIT NUTS AT SUCH LEVELS AS REFLECT THE HISTORICAL AVERAGE RELA-TIONSHIP OF FRUIT NUT SUPPORT LEVELS TO DINGLE-BERRY SUPPORT LEVELS SURING THE IMMEDIATELY PRE-CEDING ONE HUNDRED AND NINETY-NINE YEARS."

Edward J. Derwinski
Congressman, 4th, Illinois

LAUGH-IN

Senator James Buckley, Republican of New York, uses this exchange of letters between himself and his brother, author William Buckley, to thaw out audiences. He says he received this letter from a constituent:

Hon.? James Buckley, Senate Office Building, Washington, D.C.

Sir: Now that my nausea has subsided after accidentally observing your appearance on "Laugh-In" last evening, I, as one of your constituents and former admirers, am constrained to comment.

Your silly grin as the inane and vulgar questions were asked and your equally inane replies were less than worthy of a Senator of the United States.

The fact that you appeared on the program at all was an insult to the decent people whom you represent.

The disgusting episode in which you freely participated and apparently enjoyed—as an accomplice in lending your position to a disgraceful program—is an affront to the dignity of the Senate, to your family, to your church, and to your constituency. I trust that your acting the clown insured the support of the addicts of the program who undoubtedly enjoy its indecencies. I trust, too, that they are in the minority. I am . . .

April 1, 1971

Sir:

I have forwarded your letter to my brother the columnist—

108

William F. Buckley, Jr.

It was he, not I, who appeared on "Laugh-In."

I can't help but be curious as to why you consented to watch a program of which you so strongly disapprove.

Sincerely,
(signed) James L. Buckley

Happily, Bill was able to put my constituent's mind at ease with the following letter:

Dear Sir: It is typical of my brother to attempt to deceive his constituents. It was, of course, he, not I, who appeared on "Laugh-In." Just as you suspected. On the other hand, you need not worry about it. His greatest deception is as yet undiscovered. It was I, not he, who was elected to the Senate. So you see, you have nothing to worry about. You are represented in the Senate by a responsible, truthful man.

Yours, William F. Buckley, Jr.

PHOTOGENIC

When Pope John XXIII sat for his portrait by the famous photographer, Yousef Karsh, his humor was quite apparent when the Holy Father remarked, "The Lord knew from all eternity I was going to be Pope and you'd think he would have made me more photogenic."

"RUN GIOVANI"

When George Wallace was in his first term as Governor of Alabama, a black student asked to try out for the University of Alabama varsity football team. He was 6 feet 3 inches tall, weighed 220 pounds, ran the 100-yard dash in 9.3 seconds and advised the coach that he had been an All-State selection in Illinois.

COACH: "I could use a player with your potential but Governor Wallace would never permit black athletes on our varsity team."

STUDENT: "But I'm light skinned, coach. Why can't you tell him I'm an Italian?"

COACH: "We couldn't get away with it."

STUDENT: "Please give me a tryout anyway."

The coach relented and allowed the young man to participate in the first day of practice but reemphasized that he would never be able to play.

The young man threw an 80-yard pass and boomed an 80-yard punt in the opening drills and again asked the coach: "Why can't you tell the Governor that I'm an Italian?"

The coach shook his head but gave him a chance to carry the ball in a practice scrimmage.

On the first play he broke through the entire line, shook off all tacklers, and raced down the field towards a touchdown.

The coach excitedly ran down the sidelines shouting, "RUN, GIOVANNI, RUN."

Marvin L. Esch
Congressman, 2nd, Michigan

CAMPAIGN SCHOOL

At a recent campaign school for candidates, a State Representative was speaking on issues and methods of campaigning in the characteristic language of many from the southern hill country (who wish to pretend they are much less intelligent than they are). He said, "Now you campaigners must remember just one principle that I always follow as a campaigner and as a public office holder. That is you have to be 'fer everything that is good and agin everything that is bad.' Now remember, that you have to be 'fer everything that is good and agin everything that is bad.' " And then after a thoughtful pause, he added, "And you know that ain't always as easy as it sounds either."

Edwin D. Eshelman
Congressman, 16th, Pennsylvania

LOBBYING

An example of lobbying in Washington—where a woman with a wig, false eyelashes, and $100 worth of sundry camouflage can visit you in your office and lobby for "truth in packaging".

Paul Findley
Congressman, 20th, Illinois

GOING TO HELL

When he ran for Congress in 1846, Lincoln's opponent was a colorful Methodist circuit-riding minister named Peter Cartwright. Well known for his fire and brimstone preaching, Cartwright combined both politics and the pulpit. On one occasion during the campaign, Lincoln attended one of Cartwright's sermons. Cartwright thought he would make use of Lincoln's presence to bring home charges of Lincoln's atheism. During the sermon, Cartwright raised his arms in supplication and exclaimed, "All those who want to go to heaven—stand!" The entire congregation, save Lincoln, rose. Next, the preacher bellowed, "All those who want to go to hell—stand!" No one rose. Cartwright fixed his gaze on Lincoln and said, "Mr. Lincoln, you don't want to go to heaven, and you don't want to go to hell. Where do you want to go?" Lincoln rose and said, "Brother Cartwright, *I* am going to Congress."

FAT MAN'S PARTY

Pope John XXIII, whose weight was a state secret, once looked in on the Vatican's carpenter shop. To one of the workers there, a generously padded man, John said, "I see you belong to the same party that I do." "But, Holy Father, I don't belong to any party," the man replied. "Yes, you do," said Pope John, "you become a member automatically—it's the Fat Man's Party."

Gilbert Gude
Congressman, 8th, Maryland

WHEN IN DOUBT

I began a recent speech:

"Faced with the difficult problems I have been asked to address today, I am reminded of the words of James Boren, president of the Society of Professional Bureaucrats, who said: 'When in charge, ponder . . . When in trouble, delegate . . . And when in doubt, mumble . . .' Mmmmph . . . hmmmm . . . the situation is ssymmmm . . ."

BROTHER LION

Standing up to talk to a group of Democrats, I said I felt like a Christian thrown into the lion's den. (The group chuckled.) "The Christian had great faith and, despite the imminent danger of being eaten alive by the lion, he knelt and prayed. Finding himself still whole and alive, the Christian peeked through his folded, praying hands and discovered to his astonishment that the lion was kneeling down too! "Ah, Brother Lion, I'm glad to see you joining me in prayer. I'm glad to find we aren't so different after all." "Ah, Brother Christian," said the Lion, "but I'm afraid we still are. You see, *I'm* saying grace before *dinner.*"

RIVALRY

Freshman Congressman O'Bryon was feeling that he had finally "made it," and could crow a bit to a friend he had grown up with, Sol Ginsburg, now a newspaper reporter. The Congressman was crestfallen when, during his swearing in, he saw the Speaker of the House glance up and wave at somebody in the press gallery: his old friend Sol.

114

The new Congressman kept trying to upstage his journalist friend, but kept failing.

When the Congressman got an invitation—finally—from the White House, he arranged to take Sol along to show him how important he was. But the President had barely shaken hands with the Congressman before he embraced Sol and said, "Gee, Sol, I'm sorry you couldn't make that little dinner Betty and I had last week—but it's great to see you tonight."

But finally, Congressman O'Bryon got invited to Rome and had a chance to see the Pope. O'Bryon found Sol on assignment in Rome and, hoping to impress him at last, took him along to the Vatican, but then Sol disappeared. When the Pope came out to wave to O'Bryon and the rest of the crowd, there was Sol arm in arm with the Pope!

Afterwards, Sol found O'Bryon pale and prostrate on the ground. Sol found water and revived the Congressman. "I'm sorry," Sol said. "I should have warned you I'm a buddy of the Pope."

"No," said O'Bryon, "it wasn't that. What I couldn't take was when that little nun turned to me and asked, 'Who's that up there with Sol Ginsburg?' "

LIFE'S LITTLE PLEASURES

One of a Congressman's small pleasures is reading an angry letter from a person who says he'll never vote for you again—and then seeing from the address that the writer lives in another district.

POLITICAL TRUTH

A cynical friend says that the only time you can be sure a politician is telling the truth is when he is calling another politician a liar.

LAST LAUGH

A Member of Parliament tells me that the English tell a lot of jokes making fun of the Irish, but that the Irish tell this riddle:

"What's black and blue and floats in the water with it's head down?"

"An Englishman who tells Irish jokes."

Tennyson Guyer
Congressman, 4th, Ohio

POLITICS

"To get out of politics is the easiest thing I ever did; I ought to know—I've done it many times.

POLITICIANS

"In the first place, God made idiots. This was for practice. Then he made politicians."

CAMPAIGN

One day back in Ohio, I was returning to my home town of Findlay, by bus from the state capitol in Columbus. At that time I was serving in the Ohio Senate. The fellow sitting next to me was wringing his hands, turning in his seat, wiping his face, and generally was as nervous as a cat in a room full of rocking chairs. I offered my hand and said: "Fellow, what's your trouble?" He said: "Well, I've been in the penitentiary for the last five years, and I sure hate to go back home and face the people." With a real grip of his hand I said: "I have the same problem."

MEMORY

The proper memory for a politician is one that knows what to remember and what to forget.

POLITICS

"Politics is too serious a matter to be left to politicians."

116

H. John Heinz, III
Congressman, 18th, Pennsylvania

AMERICAN INDIAN

An extremely intelligent and handsome Indian from the Southwest came to Washington to testify at a committee hearing involving the affairs of his tribe. For a half-hour the Indian spoke eloquently, holding the committee members spellbound.

After the Indian completed his testimony, one of the committee members commented, "I can well appreciate the desire of your people to run their own affairs and not be wards of the government. This committee is certainly impressed with your testimony and your manner, but I find it hard to believe that you represent the typical Indian. I'm sure the tribe picked you to come here because you are superior."

"No, Congressman, that's not true," the Indian replied. "We Indians are just like other Americans—we never send our best or brightest to Washington."

Marjorie S. Holt
Congresswoman, 4th, Maryland

THE QUESTION OF LEGS

Whenever the people of Lincoln's neighborhood engaged in dispute; whenever a bet was to be decided; when they differed on points of religion or politics; when they wanted to get out of trouble, or desired advice regarding anything on the earth, below it, above it or under the sea, they went to "Abe."

Two fellows, after a hot dispute lasting some hours, over the problem as to how long a man's legs should be in proportion to the size of his body, stamped into Lincoln's office one day and put the question to him.

Lincoln listened gravely to the arguments advanced by both contestants, spent some time in "reflecting" upon the matter, and then, turning around in his chair and facing the disputants, delivered his opinion with all the gravity of a judge sentencing a fellow-being to death.

"This question has been a source of controversy," he said, slowly and deliberately, "for untold ages, and it is about time it should be definitely decided. It has led to bloodshed in the past, and there is no reason to suppose it will not lead to the same in the future.

"After much thought and consideration, not to mention mental worry and anxiety, it is my opinion, all side issues being swept aside, that a man's lower limbs, in order to preserve harmony of proportion, should be at least long enough to reach from his body to the ground."

TAIL GUNNER

When I first arrived in Washington in January, 1973, I was overwhelmed with the responsibilities facing me. But my excitement and anticipation were somewhat tempered by the terrifying tales of violent crime in our nation's capital. On the first day in office, a District of Columbia tradesman stopped by to chat. Quickly seizing the opportunity I inquired as to the true crime situation in Washington. He assured me that there was really no problem. It had been blown completely out of proportion by the media. "Washington is as safe as any city in the United States," he said decisively. Greatly relieved I began some small talk by asking him his occupation. "I'm a tail gunner on a laundry truck," he responded.

Henry J. Hyde
Congressman, 6th, Illinois

PROMISES

The young lady is already seeing her marriage counselor after only three days of marriage.

"What seems to be the trouble?" he asks.

"Oh Doctor, I'm married to a Democrat," she wails.

"Come, come," says he. "That's no reason."

"It's very frustrating," she explains. "He just sits on the bed. All I get are promises, promises, promises . . ."

BROKEN ARM

He broke his arm trying to pat himself on the back.

BORING

The speaker didn't strike oil so he kept on boring.

22-GUN SALUTE

When he was born they fired a 22-gun salute. Too bad they missed.

VACCINATED

My opponent talks a lot. He was vaccinated with a long-playing needle.

NAZI SOLDIER

Senator Hubert Humphrey was captured by some Nazi soldiers. After an hour of interrogation, his captors stated, "Senator Humphrey, ve haff veys of making you *stop* talking!"

James P. Johnson
Congressman, 4th, Colorado

INSTRUCTIONS

The first few months of every newly-elected Member of Congress are memorable. In the early transition days of the new term, my predecessor quietly called me aside and presented three numbered envelopes.

"These may be helpful," he said, "when you encounter a dilemma that appears insoluble." His advise was brief. "Open the envelopes as you need them and follow the instructions."

Some time passed before I had occasion to remember the envelopes. Producers in my District were pressing for a measure that was critically regarded by consumers. After several fitful days of indecision, I reluctantly went to my desk and retrieved envelope #1. Upon opening it, I was surprised to find just two words, "Blame me." I did, to the general acceptance of nearly all concerned.

It wasn't too long before economic pressures, lingering war-related questions, and political espionage brought the envelopes to mind once again. Since the situation seemed more severe than the first, I hoped for the best. The envelope read, "Blame the opposition party." I did, and it worked again.

Later the Congress was faced with the first presidential impeachment inquiry in more than a century. No simple solution was available. Both sides were polarized. The intensity of the moment, coupled with the successful performance of the two earlier suggestions, diminished any remaining hesitancy over calling upon my predecessor's experience. With renewed respect and understanding I read the contents of the final envelope. It said, "Prepare three envelopes."

Robert J. Lagomarsino
Congressman, 19th, California

ADVICE TO LOVELORN

Dear Ann Landers:

I am 30 years old and have two brothers. One of them is a Republican member of Congress in Washington, D.C. The other is serving a nine-year sentence in Folsom Prison for rape. My two sisters are on the streets, and my father lives off their earnings. My mother is pregnant by the neighbor next door, who refuses to marry her.

Recently, I met a charming girl. She is an ex-prostitute, single, and the mother of three lovely children.

My question is—should I tell her about my brother being a Republican?

STAY ALIVE

A Democratic precinct leader in New Jersey is driving his new Mark IV Continental through the ghetto when he is stopped by six thugs. The thugs drag him out of the car, draw a circle on the ground and tell him not to step outside the line if he wants to see the next day. Then they take rocks and sledge hammers and start to smash his car. They bash in the windows. They rip off the doors. They slash the seats. Then they overturn the car and set it afire.

They turn to the precinct chief and see that he is grinning from ear to ear. Astounded, they ask him why he's so smug after they just smashed his new car and set it afire.

"That's okay," he replies, "while you were busy I stepped over the line three times."

Robert McClory
Congressman, 13th, Illinois

ROCKEFELLER

One of my present claims to fame is that Vice President Rockefeller and I were classmates at Dartmouth College. In fact, we have many things in common. Both of us were born in the same year, both of us weighed exactly 7 lbs. 8 ozs. at birth, and both of us were initiated into the same fraternity at the same time. * * * When Nelson Rockefeller was born, he inherited his first twenty million. * * * When I was born, I weighed 7 lbs. 8 ozs.

EXPOSURE

"Smith had a brother who died of exposure. Some guy exposed him and he ended up at the end of a rope."

DEMOCRATS

"It's really terrible the way Democrats go around telling scandalous things about each other that are absolutely true."

OPEN MOUTH

One of my favorites when called upon unexpectedly to provide a few remarks is—

A politician has been defined as a person who approaches every problem with an open . . . mouth.

W. Henson Moore
Congressman, 6th, Louisiana

CONGRESS IN RECESS

In making a speech during a Congressional Recess, I point out that the country is currently safe because of the fact that Congress is in recess and can't pass any more of its usual bad legislation.

FEAR

FDR taught us that all we have to fear is fear itself, and then there is the 94th Congress.

GORILLA

A state trooper stopped a driver on the highway who had a gorilla sitting in the front seat with him. The trooper informed the driver that he could not continue indefinitely with a gorilla in the front seat as this would cause the distraction for other drivers and perhaps cause a serious accident. The state trooper then advised the driver to proceed to the next town and take the gorilla to the zoo. The driver indicated he would certainly do so. Later that afternoon the same state trooper again encounters the same driver returning, but with the gorilla still in the front seat. The state trooper stopped the driver and indignantly stated, "I thought I told you to take that gorilla to the zoo." The driver replied that he did and the gorilla enjoyed it so much, he was now on his way to take him to Disneyworld.

Carlos J. Moorhead
Congressman, 22nd, California

GOODBYE GOD

A newly elected Congressman and his family prepared to spend the last night in their old home. All the boxes were packed, and last-minute arrangements had been completed. The children had been sent to bed, and the mother was checking on them. Outside the room of her seven-year-old son she stopped to listen as she heard him praying: "God, please bless the Smiths who live up in the next block. And bless Mrs. Jones across the street who always gives us cookies. God bless Johnny and help him not to miss me too much . . ." And on and on he prayed, for all of his friends in the old neighborhood. Finally, apparently unable to think of anyone else he was leaving behind, he closed with, "Well, goodbye, God. We're going to Washington."

PRESIDENTIAL CANDIDATE

"I am convinced that the office of the President is not such a very difficult one to fill, his duties being mainly to execute the laws of Congress. Should I be chosen for this exalted position I would execute the laws of Congress as faithfully as I have always executed the orders of my superiors," said Admiral George Dewey on announcing his candidacy for the office of President of the United States, April 3, 1900.

How it must have grieved Congress that the Constitution did not allow them to elect him at once by acclamation.

Larry Pressler
Congressman, 1st, South Dakota

DOGS

One of my fondest memories occurred while doing some of my first door-to-door campaigning in 1974 when running for office for the first time in my life. It was one of those cold, drizzly April days in a rural area in the northern part of South Dakota. At that time, hardly anyone knew who I was or what I was about, but would go door-to-door with literature as candidates do.

At one particular farm house I was greeted by a rather mangy-looking, wet—but overly friendly—dog. The smelly dog was jumping up at me in a friendly fashion and to get rid of him I gave him a good slap. I went up to the door, knocked, and the lady of the house came to the door and I introduced myself and told her I was a candidate for office. She cut me off and said, "You politicians, we only see you when there's an election and we want nothing to do with you in this household." With that she slammed the door in my face.

I had that lonely feeling that only someone who has gone door-to-door can have and as I was walking back to the car, the wet puppy came running up to me and started jumping up on me again and this time I felt so lonely that I gave the dog a big hug.

It shows that a dog truly is sometimes man's best friend.

John J. Rhodes
Congressman, 1st, Arizona

GOVERNMENT RELATIONS

I think the case of two small boys illustrates pretty well the state of affairs between the Congress and the President. A mother was scolding her son: "Now Billy," she said, "you shouldn't be selfish with your toys. I've told you to let your younger brother play with them half the time."

"That's what I've been doing," said Billy. "I take the wagon going downhill—and he takes it going up."

SOCIALISM

"Under the Socialist Government more housing units have been built than ever before. Indeed—under socialism it can be proved that more hospitals have been constructed than ever before. Not only that—it can be shown that more milk has been provided to English babies than ever before. As a matter of fact—under the Socialist Government—we have witnessed the greatest increase in population in the history of the island."

At that moment, the great Winston Churchill reportedly interrupted, "Would the right honorable gentleman concede that the last statistic is due to private enterprise?"

AMERICAN HISTORY

"It has been said that there are three eras in American history—the passing of the buffalo, the passing of the Indian, and the passing of the buck."

Matthew J. Rinaldo
Congressman, 12th, New Jersey

HUBERT HUMPHREY

There I was, squeezed into a little single-engine plane with Senator Humphrey waiting for the take-off from Washington to New Jersey for a speaking engagement.

Even on the ground, the plane was being buffeted by the wind. So it was ominous when the pilot, who seemed to have difficulty seeing the dials, turned and gravely told us: "I'd better explain how you get out in an emergency . . ."

But trust Hubert. He nudged me and piped up: "Oh, don't worry, Matt; if anything goes wrong just follow me—I'll be out of the plane in a flash!"

ELECTION RETURNS

In New Jersey, Chuck Wepner, the Hoboken boxer who went 14 rounds with Muhammed Ali, gave me the secret of persistent Democratic victories in his hometown elections.

"The last time somebody broke into the mayor's office in Hoboken," said Wepner, "they found next year's election returns . . ."

ON THE FLOOR?

Capitol Hill terminology must have quite a few constituents puzzled.

Imagine the bewilderment of a woman who telephoned and asked for me, only to be told: "Oh, the Congressman is on the floor."

"What's he doing on the floor?" she asked in obvious bewilderment.

"Oh," said my secretary, "he's voting."

"On the floor?" queried the caller. "I thought he voted in Congress . . ."

QUICK FUN

Then there's the time when a newspaper columnist rushed up and exclaimed: "Matt—I need something funny for my column and I need it in a hurry."

"It's not easy to think of something funny on the spur of the moment," I told him. "Can you?"

"Easy!" he answered. "I heard a comment just a few minutes ago about a Senator. It goes: 'I won't say he drinks, but they're going to have to get a liquor license to bury him!' "

Herman T. Schneebeli
Congressman, 17th, Pennsylvania

IDENTITY

Someone with a name like Schneebeli had better get used to having it misspelled, mispronounced, or simply forgotten. However, it can be rather unnerving when such things happen during the heat of a political campaign.

During the spring of 1960, I was running in a special election for a vacant Congressional seat; this was my first venture into politics as a candidate. The contest was being touted as a possible early indication of how things might go in the approaching Presidential election.

Name recognition was a necessary goal, and a large political rally was scheduled in a county in which I was not well known. Three Republican Congressmen from outside the state attended, emphasizing the importance being placed on the contest.

After the usual preliminaries, the local county GOP chairman began introducing me. I hadn't met him before, and was flattered by his praise. After a while, however, as the platitudes flowed on, it got to be rather embarrassing and the audience became restless. It was evident that something was wrong.

Finally, the chairman took a dramatic pause, ostensibly reaching for a glass of water. While doing so, he whispered to the state chairman, "Just what is this guy's name, anyhow?" Obviously, he did not notice the live microphone near him on the table.

When the laughing stopped and my name was given to him, it must have been remembered, since I carried the county and won the election by a narrow margin.

Incidentally, it's pronounced SHNAY-blee.

Richard T. Schulze
Congressman, 5th, Pennsylvania

CHANGING PARTIES

One of my favorite stories told to me by Rogers Morton:

There lived in a small West Virginia town an insurance man who was the mainstay of the local Republican Party. He was 89 years old and had a very active life—in his office each day at 8:30 and quite involved in local affairs.

His physical well-being started to deteriorate rapidly so he went to see his doctor. "Jim," his doctor told him, "you have had a full and rewarding life and all I can tell you is that the end is near. You have about two months to live and I would suggest that you go up to your cabin in the mountains and sit in your rocking chair and enjoy your last days."

Well, the man took the doctor's advice. One day close to the end of the two months Jim, who was bedridden by this time, was being visited by his son and some other relatives when he startled all by asking his son to go to the county court house and bring back the registrar so that he could change his registration from Republican to Democrat. Surrounding his bed, the family pleaded with him not to do such a thing and finally his son said: "Dad, why would you, the man who started the Republican Party in this town, who has seen it grow from infancy to the point where we now control the Court House and are now the Majority Party in the county, who has attended every Republican benefit affair, and fundraising dinner ever put on, who is known as "Mr. Republican" in this area—why would you want to change your registration from Republican to Democrat?"

The old man turned and said: "Well, son, the doc was up here yesterday and told me that I only have a few days left, and if somebody has to die I'd rather it be one of them!"

Keith G. Sebelius
Congressman, 1st, Kansas

FARMER

Then there was the time an Eastern colleague of mine in the Congress was visiting in western Kansas. He pointed out with great satisfaction the number of wealthy farmers who were driving luxury cars.

That prompted a farmer to say: "Oh that's nothing. Most of the farmers around here buy cars that even have a glass partition between the front and back seats."

Puzzled, the Congressman said, "Why would you want a glass partition between the seats?"

"Well, you see," the farmer replied, "that keeps the hogs from licking the back of your neck when you take them to market."

SENATOR DIRKSEN

Former Senator Everett McKinley Dirksen, described as "the wizard of ooze, who marinates his tonsils with honey" and "born with a golden thesaurus in his mouth," once said, "I must use beautiful words, I never know when I might have to eat them."

WILL ROGERS

As Will Rogers said, politics is a promising profession, but it is not one of the performing arts.

CONFERENCE

A conference is a gathering of people who individually can do nothing about a problem but, coming together as a group, can determine that nothing can be done.

POLLUTION

Pollution has been much in the news. Last year it was water pollution, this year air pollution. Next year the focus will be on political pollution, a condition in which the air is filled with speeches and vice versa.

BETTER MOUSETRAP

This inventor decided he would build a better mousetrap, so he took the rather large, complicated contraption to Washington to get the approval and blessing of the Chief Bureaucrats.

They asked him, "How does it work?"

He said, "Well, you see this red carpet coming out of the hole in the box. The mouse sees that red carpet and feels he's welcome. He walks on that red carpet and once he gets inside, the floor is on an incline and there's a tiny, specially built mouse skate. He jumps on that mouse skate and slides to the bottom of the incline where there is a little block. He smells some cheese, so he sticks his head over the block where there is some cheese hanging from a string. He bites the cheese and when he does this, he pulls the string and lets a big hatchet come down and it chops his head off!"

The Chief Bureaucrat says, "Well, I'm sorry fellow, but I can't approve that. First of all, the red carpet sticking out the way it does—somebody might trip over it and the Product Safety Commission certainly could not approve that. Also, the material of the carpet is flammable and under the Flammable Materials Act, that certainly could not be approved. And that skate—it has no braking system on it, so we certainly can't have that skate there. And the cheese is not wrapped, so the Food and Drug Administration couldn't have that cheese there. And, my goodness, OSHA could never let an axe like that be falling! Someone might stick his finger in there and get it chopped off!"

The inventor was upset and a little downfallen, so he went home and re-did the invention and brought it back. The Chief Bureaucrat asked, "How does it work?", and the inventor explained it thusly:

"Well, first of all, the carpet doesn't extend out there", and the bureaucrat said, "That's fine."

"Then, the carpet is no longer made of flammable material," to which the bureaucrat replied, "That's good."

"Then we've eliminated the skate and the incline, so the mouse will just have to walk," and the bureaucrat said, "That's good too."

Then the inventor got to the block, and said, "We've just got a hacksaw blade fixed permanently in the block, "and the bureaucrat said, "That's OK—that works pretty good too, but where's the cheese? You've eliminated the cheese! How in the world are you going to catch the mouse?"

"Very simple, The mouse enters the hole, walks down the carpet, gets to the block, looks over, doesn't see any cheese, sees that string hanging down, and, shaking his head back and forth, says, "Where's the cheese?" as he looks around, and saws off his head!"

Joe Skubitz
Congressman, 5th, Kansas

PUBLIC SPEAKING

On the two-hour flight back to his District for an important speech to a large audience, the Freshman Congressman had worriedly studied and silently rehearsed his speech. Landing at his home town airport, he glanced nervously at his watch. Right on time. Feeling more self-assured and confident his speech would be well-received, he headed for the men's room. Turning away from the lavatory to the electric dryer, he started to press the button, only to stare at a bold, hand-lettered sign which read, "Push button: hear your Congressman speak."

KING CAUCUS

It's interesting to think back to the times right after the 1974 elections and at the beginning of the 94th Congress, and to remember what people like George Meany and Speaker Carl Albert were saying. Those were the days when we were hearing all about the "veto-proof Congress," and that with such a large Democratic majority, there would be no problem at all in passing the Democratic programs.

Yes, it's particularly interesting to think back to those times and to remember those words—especially when you look at what happened during the last two days before the August recess. Why, the Democrats had to try six times before they could muster enough votes even to get a majority just to agree to adjourn.

DECISION

The man awoke to find a note on his wife's pillow, informing him that she was leaving and taking the children. He called his office to explain that his ulcers were acting up again and that he wouldn't be in that day. He was told it was perfectly alright because his termination notice and severence pay had just gone out in the mail.

Since the man's wife had taken the car, he walked the five miles through the snow to the bank. The teller was happy to see him. Now he wouldn't have to waste a stamp on the overdraft notice. The loan officer was also pleased. He much preferred to discuss mortgage foreclosures in his own office.

The visit to the doctor didn't take long. After all, what does a country doctor know about encephalytis? And the fall on the ice wasn't nearly as painful as the realization that he had lost his key and the only way into the house was through the coal chute.

Sitting alone in the dark and cold, the man considered his situation. Finally, he slowly opened the desk drawer and took out his gun. Suddenly, he saw the small card: "CALL US BEFORE YOU PULL THE TRIGGER. SUICIDE CENTRAL: 601-5843."

A voice answered. The girl on the other end of the line heard him out, occasionally murmuring with sympathy. "I'm new at this," she said. "I'll have to consult my colleagues. I'll call you right back. Please don't do anything. Please wait."

The man slumped on the hard-back chair, the gun dangling from his frost-bitten fingers. The telephone rang. A fleeting light of hope crossed his face. He picked up the receiver.

"Sorry to have taken so long," the voice said, "but I wanted to give all the details to my colleagues. We've discussed your problems from every angle. We all agree that you have made the right decision."

Floyd Spence
Congressman, 2nd, South Carolina

MR. DEVIL

The preacher in the old country church was just getting into the spirit of his sermon. With a great deal of emotion, he was admonishing his congregation for indulging in the evils of drinking, smoking and carousing with women.

About this time, a man could be seen ambling down the old country road which passed by the church. He was returning from a masquerade party where he had gone dressed as the devil. He had obviously enjoyed the festivities to the fullest. About that time, it started to rain, and he sought shelter in the nearest building—the church.

As he reached the doorway, a great flash of lightning struck behind him. The congregation turned to see the devil himself framed in the doorway of the church. As we say in the law, you can imagine the consternation of the worshipers therein! Everyone rushed to escape by any available means—through windows and doors—and some passages which had not existed moments before.

Only one rather large lady could not find an opening, so she approached the devil rather boldly and addressed him face to face. "Mr. Devil," she said, "I've been a member of this congregation for near-on to 45 years. But I've been on your side all the time!"

Alan Steelman
Congressman, 5th, Texas

DIPLOMACY

A Congressman went home each summer for 20 years for an annual town hall meeting. One exasperated constituent, after asking a question and getting an evasive answer said, "I've been coming to hear you for 20 years and I haven't gotten a straight answer yet. Will you even tell me your favorite color?" The Congressman paused reflectively and said, "Yes, it's plaid."

BURGLARS

President Cleveland was awakened by his wife who said, "Grover, Grover, wake up. There are burglars in the house." President Cleveland rolled over and drowsily said, "No, dear, there may be burglars in the Senate, but not in the House."

FEDERAL GOVERNMENT

"The Federal Government is getting harder and harder to support in the style to which it has become accustomed."

WASHINGTON, D. C.

"Washington, D.C., is a city where many a politician is waiting to be discovered, and many are afraid they might be."

UNEMPLOYED

Mrs. Smith had four sons. The first was a lawyer, the second was a politician, the third was a university graduate, and the fourth was also unemployed.

CONGRESSMAN

The little girl was overheard to say, "My father was a Congressman until he lost the election; now he has a job."

NERVOUS BREAKDOWN

Congressman Smith's wife was obviously very happy the day her friend came to visit her. "Why are you so happy?" she asked. Mrs. Smith replied, "I just received wonderful news. My husband had a nervous breakdown and the doctor is sending us to Palm Springs, California."

Steve Symms
Congressman, 1st, Idaho

PROFESSIONALS

Three professional men were arguing over whose profession was the oldest. They were a doctor, an architect and a politician. The doctor finally said, "I've got proof that mine is the oldest profession. The Bible tells us that God made Woman from Adam's rib. That was a medical act and thus my profession, medicine, is the oldest."

"Wait a minute," the architect said, "before that happened, it says in the Bible that God made order out of all the chaos in the world. That's architecture pure and simple, so that proves that architecture is the oldest profession."

At that point, the politician settled it once and for all: "Gentlemen—where do you think all that chaos came from?"

Gene Taylor
Congressman, 7th, Missouri

LION'S CAGE

One of my favorite and most effective stories concerns the man who had fallen on hard times. He hadn't worked in months and was desperately looking for a job, willing to do anything, willing to work for any price.

As a last resort he went to the director of the local zoo in hopes of finding work. He offered to feed the tigers, sweep out the cages, anything that was required of him.

The director thought for a moment and then said, "You know, I might possibly have something after all. Last week our gorilla died. It was probably the biggest attraction that we had because literally thousands of school children use to visit the zoo each year just to watch the gorilla swing from limb to limb. They will be severely disappointed if they come to visit and we have no gorilla."

The director said, "We have preserved the animal's skin, and if you will put it on and get in the cage I'll pay you $25.00 a week. In that way, you'll have work and the children will not be disappointed."

The man donned the suit, climbed into the cage and gingerly started to climb the tree. A crowd of children gathered around to watch. As the man climbed higher they became more excited and began to clap their hands and shout and laugh.

Encouraged, the man began to really perform, he started to swing from branch to branch. The more the children applauded the harder he tried and the higher he swung. Suddenly, as he was at the height of a swing the branch broke and his momentum carried him over the fence right into the middle of the lion's cage."

As the man looked around trying to find a way out, he saw the lion begin to advance in his direction. Letting out a yell he started trying to climb the wall. He was screaming at the top of his voice, "Get me out of here, this wasn't in the deal." At that moment, the lion caught up with him, grabbed him by the neck and jerked his head toward him.

With his mouth close to the man's ear the lion whispered, "Shut up you fool or we'll both be out of a job."

Guy Vander Jagt
Congressman, 9th, Michigan

HOW TO WIN ELECTIONS

Mayor Daley, Lyndon Johnson, and Everett Dirkson were flying on a plane across the Atlantic. The plane developed engine trouble and landed kerplop in the ocean. The three of them emerged from the icy water clinging to one tiny life raft. There was room for only one aboard the life raft and the water was so cold, it was clear that only one would survive and the other two would be lost. They began to quarrel who the one would be who would survive, but Lyndon Johnson said, "Come now, let us reason together," and sure enough soon a concensus developed. They agreed that they would decide the issue the democratic way and they would vote by secret ballot and the one who received the most votes would be the one who would climb aboard the life raft and survive. So they voted and when they counted the votes, the results were: one for Everett Dirksen, one vote for Lyndon Johnson, and 28 votes for Mayor Daley of Chicago.

HOW TO LOSE FRIENDS

Shortly after a bruising battle regarding whether the Coast Guard cutter MACKINAW would be stationed in Grand Haven in my Congressional District, or in Cheboygan in Congressman Phil Ruppe's Congressional District, and during which emotions on all sides had run high, I was attending the National Coast Guard Festival in Grand Haven. Grand Haven and I had lost our struggle and the MACKINAW had cruised down from its home port of Cheboygan to participate in the festivities. After Coast Guard Festival parade, I headed a group of dignitaries on a tour of the MACKINAW.

All parties concerned were now anxious to show that no hard feelings remained—that we were all on the same team and that we all were strong proponents of a vital U.S. Coast Guard. That included the Captain of the MACKINAW. His efforts to show complete reconciliation knew no bounds. He took my five-year-old daughter and my wife and me into the Captain's quarters, and in efforts far beyond the call of duty, entertained by performing magic tricks and even standing on his head for her entertainment. By the time he escorted us to the gangplank to say farewell, he had completely won my daughter's heart and mine as well. But he blew it all with his farewell remark: "It was such a thrill, Congressman Vander Jagt, to have you and your wife and lovely granddaughter on board the MACKINAW!"

LIAR

Lincoln told this story about one of his severest critics:

"He's the biggest liar in Washington. He reminds me of an old fisherman who had the reputation for stretching the truth. He got a pair of scales and insisted on weighing every fish he caught in front of witnesses. One day a doctor borrowed his scales to weigh a new baby. The baby weighed 47 pounds."

G. William Whitehurst
Congressman, 2nd, Virginia

NEW DEALER

A young man and his grandfather were shaking hands as they left church one Sunday. As they came to one gentleman, the youth said, "Grandfather, I want you to meet the new deacon." The old man, who was hard of hearing, snapped, "Did you say New Dealer?" "No, no, Granddad," the young man replied, "he's the son of a bishop." "They all are!" his grandfather roared.

Larry Winn, Jr.
Congressman, 3rd, Kansas

SCHOOL GIRL

Sometime a few years ago, I was scheduled to address two combined fifth grade classes in an elementary school in my Congressional District. As I entered the school, a few minutes late, a little girl came up to me and said, "Aren't you Larry Winn?" I said, "yes." Then she said, taking me by the hand, "Won't you please come with me." I said, "Honey, aren't you a little small for being in the fifth grade?" She said she was in the first grade and I told her I had come to speak to two fifth grade classes who were waiting for me. Again she repeated, "Won't you please come with me." and started leading me down another hall toward her room. I finally balked and asked why she was so insistant on my going to her class. She answered with all sincerity, "Because we're having 'show and tell'."

John W. Wydler
Congressman, 5th, New York

TAX COLLECTOR

Herbert Hoover, as President, returned all of his salary to the government. In those days this was quite an event. Today, we all return out salaries to the government and nobody thinks much of it. The younger generation will soon find out that the "Man From Uncle" is the tax collector.

GOOD ENOUGH

When I find a reactionary outlook to a problem, I tell the story of the person who insists on having the King James version of the Bible, saying, "If it was good enough for the Apostle Paul, it's good enough for me."

THE 94TH (CONGRESS) PSALM

The politician is my Shepherd . . . I am in want.
He maketh me to lie down on park benches.
He leadeth me beside the still factories.
He restoreth the dole.
He mis-leadeth me in the paths of confusion for the Party's
    sake.
Yea, tho I walk through the shadow of depression, I anticipate
    no recovery, for He is with me.
He prepareth a reduction in my salary in the presence of mine
    enemies.
He annointeth my income with taxes; my expense runneth over.

Surely, taxes and inflation shall follow me all the days of my
life.
And I shall dwell in a mortgaged home forever.

Chalmers P. Wylie
Congressman, 15th, Ohio

OUTSIDE OF LOCK 77

When I was Assistant Attorney General of Ohio, I was assigned to try a workmen's compensation case. The applicant for workmen's compensation was a young lady who was claiming death benefits under the Ohio Workmen's Compensation Act for the death of her husband. There was no question that the person who was killed was killed in the course of and arising out of his employment. The legal question was whether this young lady was his wife at the time of his death.

Ohio is one of the five states where common law marriage is still possible. The test is establishing a reputation for being husband and wife in the community.

The young lady's lawyer did a fine job of establishing that when she went out in the community she referred to him as her husband and then when he went out in the community he referred to her as his wife, that they had lived together as husband and wife for about two years on a houseboat tied up in the Ohio River just outside of Lock 77.

On cross-examination I went through some of the same questions without being able to shake the young lady's story. I did determine that they had a child. I asked the young lady: "Now, I understand there is a child born of this union." She said: "Yes, we had a kid." I said. "Was the child born on the houseboat?" She said, "Yes, it was on the houseboat." I said, as my key question. "The child was born out of wedlock, wasn't it?" Very indignantly and without hesitation, she looked me straight in the eye and said, "Hell no. Mister, I just told you it was born outside of Lock 77.

The sequal to the story is that she received the full death award.

C. W. Bill Young
Congressman, 6th, Florida

"LIKEE SPEECHEE?"

One of the pleasant things about being a Member of Congress is the many different people you get to meet. As an example, I recently had the opportunity to attend an international banquet at the United Nations. This banquet was to honor certain people who had made great contributions to humanity in the field of education, medicine, health research, and so forth.

I was seated at one of those big round tables and the fellow sitting next to me was obviously of oriental descent. In an attempt to strike up a conversation and to be friendly with him—when the soup course was served, I looked over at him, smiled and said, likee soupee?

His reaction was sort of strange—he frowned and made no verbal response at all. But, I was determined to get a dialogue going and to communicate with him and to establish a friendship. So, when the main course was served and we began to eat, I again looked over at him and said, likee steakee?

His reaction was the same—he frowned, looked at me rather strangely and made no other response.

After the dinner was over and the dishes were cleared and the speeches were begun—the awards were made—and finally, they came to the main award of the evening to the individual who had made the greatest contribution to humanity in the last 12 months. With a fine introduction, none other than my Chinese friend sitting next to me, stood up and approached the rostrum.

For 10 minutes he spoke in beautiful English, using words that I had never even heard and accepted his award, speaking very intelligently of what he had been doing and what he planned to do. As he stood at the rostrum accepting his applause—just as the applause died out—he looked over at me, grinned and said, "Likee speechee?"

Don W. Adams
Republican National Committee, Illinois

EPITAPH

An epitaph on a tombstone in a small Southern Illinois cemetary reads, "Here lies a Democrat and an honest man."

Our question is, "How did they get two guys in the same grave?"

Frederick Biebel
Republican National Committee, Connecticut

MICROPHONE

A prominent political leader, while delivering the principal speech at an important dinner, was repeatedly interrupted by the whining feedback of the rostrum microphone. Finally, an electrician was summoned from somewhere in the bowels of the hotel and, as the speaker stepped back, the workman crawled underneath the rostrum. He reappeared shortly with a self-satisfied smile on his face and boomed into the now-perfect microphone, "There was nothing wrong here except for a screw loose on the rostrum."

TOASTMASTER

A governor and a U.S. Senator were the scheduled speakers at a major political banquet. The inept toastmaster, after having stumbled through introductions of head table guests and after having unsuccessfully tried to ad lib a few jokes, finally took from his pocket a well-worn script extolling the next speaker as a "man of the people", a "man of decision", a "man whose record needs no apology", a "man whose every fiber is dedicated to the people's welfare", and a "man who stands above all others in accomplishment, ability and achievement".

He finished reading his script, then abruptly turned to the head table and asked: "Which one of you guys wants to go first?"

WAITER

The vacationing Governor and his family were giving the resort staff a particularly hard time. He complained about his room, the valet service, the recreational facilities, the food, the service and the caliber of entertainment in the cocktail lounge. When he swung around in his chair suddenly and caused an approaching waiter to spill a bit of a drink on his wife's shoulder, the Governor fairly exploded: "If you lived in my state, I'd have you committed to the institution for idiots."

The waiter echoed the sentiments of the entire hotel staff with his retort: "If I lived in your state, Governor, I'd let you."

Mrs. Harold B. Barton
Republican National Committee, Kentucky

KENTUCKY

One of my favorite toasts to Kentucky with its description of Kentucky politics was made by a judge more than 75 years ago. The last verse reads:

"The song birds are the sweetest in Kentucky;
The thoroughbreds are fleetest in Kentucky;
Mountains tower proudest,
Thunder peals the loudest,
The landscape is the grandest,
And politics the damnedest in Kentucky."

Anyone that has been active in Kentucky politics knows this to be true . . . the political climate hasn't changed much in those 75 years.

BEAUTY AND CHARM

Do you know the difference in a beautiful woman and a charming woman? A beautiful woman is one that you notice, and a charming woman is one that notices you!

WOMEN IN POLITICS

Over the years, I have been asked to participate in workshops, seminars, etc., to encourage women to become active in politics, and particularily in campaigns. I always stress how invaluable they are—so dependable, dedicated to their beliefs, thorough and sincere. I'd rather have one woman helping me in a campaign than ten men. You know how the old saying goes . . . "The cock croweth, but the hen delivereth the goods!"

157

Mrs. Concepcion C. Barrett
Republican National Committee, Guam

CALL GIRL

Senator Concepción Barrett became a member of the 'Committee on Call' and during an interview with the Press, the reporter asked her, "Senator, what are your duties as a member of the Committee on Call?" The lady lawmaker replied, "I'm a CALL GIRL". Republican National Committeeman, Pete Perez, remarked, "Oh, Senator Barrett, you finally turned professional!"

I'M A TERRITORIAL

Senator Concepcion Barrett was asked if she was a Republican. She answered, "How can I be a Republican? I'm not from a republic—I'm a Territorial from the Territory of Guam."

Mrs. Grace Boulton
Republican National Committee, Oklahoma

HANG ONE

Senator Don Ferrell, Republican leader in the Oklahoma Senate in 1972 and '73, campaigning for re-election in his district in central Oklahoma, drove by a farm house one day and stopped to visit with an old man sitting in his rocking chair on the porch. After introducing himself and commenting on the weather and the crops, Don asked if the man had ever voted for any Republicans. The farmer rocked and thought for several seconds, then answered: "Yea, I voted for a Republican once. About twenty years ago I was on a jury and I voted to hang one."

OPEN RANGE

A Democrat politician from Oklahoma City, running his first statewide race, was scheduled to speak at a meeting in the southeastern part of the state. He was late arriving and the meeting was already in progress when he entered and asked hurriedly of a local office-holder what the burning issue was in that part of the state. The answer was "open range." (For city slickers, "open range" is the practice of allowing livestock to roam free without fences to keep them in.) Just then the politician was introduced and without the vaguest knowledge of the subject gave a stirring oration in support of "open range," for which he was wildly applauded. When the applause died down his parting remark was: "I'm sorry I was late tonight, folks, but I ran into a cow crossing the road. I sure wish you folks would fence in those animals."

Edward Brennan
Republican National Committee, Hawaii

ETHICS

A congressman, who had been under fire by the news media for unethical practices, was asked by his teenaged son what specifically did they mean by "ethics". The congressman replied that it was very difficult to define, but he would attempt to cite an example.

He said, "Let's assume that my partner and I own a retail store. A customer comes in and buys $5.00 worth of goods and gives me a $20.00 bill. I give him change for ten. Ethics is "Should I tell my partner?"

Mrs. Myrene R. Brewer
Republican National Committee, Utah

DIE HAPPY

My father was an early pioneer physician and surgeon in Utah. One of his favorite experiences is as follows: He had operated on an old man for strangulated hernia. The bowel was gangrenous, and a portion of it had to be resected. The patient was in poor condition after the operation and it was evident he could not recover. When my father visited him the next day he realized the man was failing fast. The patient, who was hard to hearing, motioned for him to come nearer; and bending over the sick man, the doctor expected to hear a last message for the family. But to his surprise, the patient asked weakly, "Are you a Republican?" "Yes," answered my father reassuringly. The old man smiled appreciatively. The reply seemed to please him and he whispered, "That is good." A few hours later he was dead.

FIRST VOTE

A grandson on the occasion of my father's 100th birthday quoted from a letter he had received from his grandfather on his birthday; 1947—November 7th "You will be 21 years of age in a few days, a man with your own right—too young to vote this year but you can vote for a Republican President next."

PRAY FOR PEOPLE

Small boy, a student of government, seeking information from his father, "Daddy what does the chaplain in the Congress do? Does he pray for the Congress?" Father—"No, son, the chaplain looks at the Congress and prays for the people."

William C. Cramer
Republican National Committee, Florida

MAKING MONEY

"There are hundreds of ways to make money," said a politician, "but only one honest way." "What's that?" asked his opponent in debate. "Aha," retorted the first, "I thought you wouldn't know!"

FRIENDS

A man ran for sheriff in a small western town, but he received a sound beating at the polls, getting only a mere 125 votes out of a total of 10,000. The day after the big election, he strolled down Main Street with two guns strapped about his mid-section. Confronted by a group of puzzled and indignant citizens, he was asked, "See here . . . you have no right to carry those guns. After all, you aren't the one who was elected sheriff." "Listen here, my friend," he replies, "A man with no more friends than I've got in this community needs to carry a gun!"

CONGRESSIONAL ESTEEM

As an indication of the high regard that most people have for members of Congress these days, I am reminded of the Congressman from Pennsylvania, who used to travel on a train that occasionally carried convicts from an insane asylum from the northern part of Pennsylvania to the southern part. The Congressman inadvertently got into the same car in which some 20 members of the insane asylum were seated. The conductor went through the train checking up on his passengers.

When he came to the convicts, he was going down the line

counting them, "One, two, three, four, five, six, seven, eight," and he stopped at the seat in which the Congressman was sitting and said, "Who are you?" He said, "I am the Congressman from the 10th District of Pennsylvania." "Nine, ten, eleven."

ALBEN BARKLEY'S SPEECH

One of my old favorite stories is the one former Vice President Alben Barkley used to tell about a friend's comment after one of his speeches.

Barkley had finished speaking before a large audience when a friend approached to ask if he would mind some minor criticism. The Vice President said that he would, of course, welcome any criticism.

"Well, Mr. Vice President—First of all, your speech was too long."

The Vice President nodded his head and agreed. "This is true I guess it was."

"Secondly," the friend continued, "you read your speech."

The Vice President again agreed and begged pardon in that he did not have time to commit the speech to memory; whereafter, his critic added, quickly, "and beside that, it wasn't worth reading."

David R. Forward
Republican National Committee, Maryland

IT'S A TOUGH LIFE

"I'll run over and pick up my unemployment check, and then go over to the U and see what's holding up my check on my Federal Education Grant, and then pick up our food stamps. Meanwhile you go to the Free VD Clinic and check up on your tests, then pick up my new glasses at the Health Center, then go to the Welfare Department and try to increase our eligibility limit again. Later we'll meet at the Federal Building for the mass demonstration against the stinking, rotten establishment."

Richard C. Frame
Republican National Committee, Pennsylvania

DOGS

I recall an incident at a polling place in Philadelphia: The Democratic Party Committeeman was there and had with him his two poodles. The Republican Committeeman, obviously from a less affluent part of the election division also had his pet, a dog of mixed parentage. As time went on, the Republican dog approached the two pedigreed poodles and asked them their names. They replied, Mimi . . . . . M-I-M-I and Fifi . . . . . F-I-F-I. The Republican dog then volunteered that his name was Fido . . . . . P-H-Y-D-E-A-U-X.

CAB DRIVER

The Republican and Democratic State Committee Chairmen had occasion to share a taxicab from the local airport to an intersection near their respective offices.

When they got out of the cab, both tipped the driver two dollars and he drove off.

The Democratic State Chairman said to the Republican State Chairman, "Usually, when I tip, I tell the driver that I'm the Democratic State Chairman and urge him to vote Democratic."

The Republican Chairman replied, "That's funny, when I get out of a taxi, I usually don't tip at all—I tell the driver that I'm the Democratic State Chairman and urge him to vote Democratic."

Mrs. M. Stanley Ginn
Republican National Committee, Missouri

WOMEN

Once a lady suffragist was lecturing on the many ways in which women have suffered. She said, "Women have suffered in an thousand ways."

And the small man in the front row stood it as long as he was able. He arose and shouted back at her, "Wal, Lady, there's one way in which they ain't never suffered."

The lecturer glared at him and said, "And, my good man, what is that?"

The man gathered all his courage and replied, "They ain't never suffered in silence."

John H. Haugh
Republican National Committee, Arizona

GOVERNMENT SPENDING

This true story demonstrated the frequent frustration of the campaigning politician.

My friend, running for re-election to the Missouri legislature, encountered an old supporter who said he could no longer vote for him.

"You spent too much money," he noted, "like building that palace for the Highway Patrol headquarters."

"We have to have a good patrol," my friend protested, "Look at the good they do. Think of all the accidents the patrol *has prevented!*"

The complaining voter quickly raised his eyes and ordered, "Name one."

IDENTITY

Senator Fannin entered the world of politics by running for Governor of the State of Arizona, serving three terms, and then became the U.S. Senator from Arizona when Barry Goldwater ran for the presidency and refused to run for two offices at the same time.

After a year or so in office in Washington, U.S. Senator Fannin returned to Phoenix on one occasion and picked up a young hitch-hiker as he was going from one speaking engagement to another. The young man sat in silence for quite a while and then finally said, "Weren't you Governor Fannin?" The Senator replied, "Yes", and before he was able to say anything further the young man brightly asked, "Whatever happened to you?"

Mrs. James F. Hooper
Republican National Committee, Mississippi

GOOD CANDIDATE—BUT

During this same election there was a rally in the heart of the "yellow dog" Democrat part of our state. I was to meet the candidate and asked a friend to meet me there who was the niece of the old political boss of the county and knew about everyone there. He went to the rally with us and listened to our candidate with great interest. After the rally was over he told us that our candidate was a handsome young man who had brains and he really liked everything about him and would like to help him. We were thrilled. And then he leaned over to my friend and whispered, "I wouldn't tell this to a soul but did you know that someone told me he was a Republican?"

TWO PARTY SYSTEM

In 1963 Mississippi was still very much of a one-party state. The first Republican candidate for Governor called my husband and asked if he would speak for him at a rally at the Bailey box in a rural area of Oktibeha County. My husband told him that he was not a very good speaker and asked that he find someone else. The candidate insisted that there would not be a very big crowd and said that he only wanted to be represented and that it did not matter about a good speech. When we arrived there were pickup trucks on each side of the highway for miles and there was a tremendous crowd. My husband climbed up on the flat bed truck that was used as a platform and gave a great speech about the two-party system and what it would do for our state.

When the election returns came in we found that my husband

was a better speaker than he had thought because 60% of the votes in that box had been thrown out. 60% of the people had voted for a two-party system in our state—they had voted for both candidates for Governor, for the Democrat and the Republican.

Cyril M. Joly, Jr.
Republican National Committee, Maine

ODE TO THE WELFARE STATE

Father, must I go to work?
    No, my lucky son,
We're living now on easy street,
    On dough from Washington.
We've left it up to Uncle Sam,
    So don't get exercised.
Nobody has to give a damn,
    We've all been subsidized.
But if Sam treats us all so well,
    And feeds us milk and honey,
Please, Daddy, tell me what the Hell
    He's going to use for money.
Don't worry, Bub, there's not a hitch
    In this here noble plan.
He simply soaks the filthy rich
    And helps the common man.
But Father, won't there come a time
    When they have run out of cash
And we have left them not a dime
    When things will go to smash?
My faith in you is shrinking, son,
    You nosy little brat.
You do too damn much thinking, son,
    To be a Democrat.

John R. Linnell
Republican National Committee, Maine

TAKE IT ALL

1964 was as poor a year for Republicans in Maine as it was most every other place. This fact did not sit very well with one gas station owner who awoke the day following the election to find Democrats holding every elective office in the county.

As he was reflecting on this state of events a car festooned with bumper stickers calling for the election of various Democrats to local office pulled into the yard.

The driver rolled down the window and said, "Say old fella, can I take this road to Augusta?" After a pause the reply came, "You might as well, you've taken everything else."

ROAD DIRECTIONS

The giving of directions is sometimes described as Maine's second favorite sport. (The first being taking down all the signs that say "Used Furniture" just before the tourists arrive for the summer and putting up the one that says "Antiques.")

A Democratic candidate for State Senate discovered this when he was heading for a meeting in Skohegan and came to a fork in the road with each branch of the fork carrying a sign and arrow that said "Skowhegan". Properly perplexed he pulled to the side of the highway to ask directions.

"Does it make any difference which road I take to Skowhegan?" he asked of the farmer he saw heading for the back pasture. The farmer looked at the candidate and replied evenly, "Not to me it don't."

George N. McMath
Republican National Committee, Virginia

WELFARE DEPARTMENT LETTERS

Here are examples of unclear writing. These are sentences taken from actual letters received by the Welfare Department in application for support.

- I am forwarding my marriage certificate and six children. I had seven but one died which was baptized on a half sheet of paper.

- Mrs. Jones has not had any clothes for a year and has been visited regularly by the clergy.

- I am glad to report that my husband who is missing is dead.

- This is my eighth child. What are you going to do about it?

- Please find for certain if my husband is dead. The man I am now living with can't eat or do anything until he knows.

- I am very much annoyed to find that you have branded my son illiterate. This is a dirty lie as I was married a week before he was born.

- I am forwarding my marriage certificate and my three children, one of which is a mistake as you can see.

- I have no children as yet as my husband is a truck driver and works day and night.

- In accordance with your instructions, I have given birth to twins in the enclosed envelope.

- I want my money as quick as I can get it. I have been in bed with my doctor for two weeks and he doesn't do me any good. If things don't improve I will have to send for another doctor.

●   I was sick last week, I couldn't report, so I called the doctor he said that I had a bad cold, asked what I was doing for it, I said coughing and blowing my nose.

Edwin G. Middleton
Republican National Committee, Kentucky

KENTUCKY POLITICIAN

Once upon a time a Kentucky politician, who was quite an orator, was making a speech, out of state. He was just getting warmed up, after talking about 45 minutes, and his throat became parched and his voice cracked to the extent that he turned from the microphone and asked the master of ceremonies to please furnish him with a drink. Almost immediately a tray with a large crystal clear pitcher of ice water and a glass was presented to him, whereupon, the distinguished speaker drew himself up to his full length and looked with disdain upon the master of ceremonies, and said, "Sir, I am from Kentucky."

Mrs. Isabel C. Moberly
Republican National Committee, Montana

TELEPHONE CONVERSATION

The six-term Congressman, having but recently been narrowly returned to his seat in a cliff-hanger election after an exhausting, bone-wearying campaign in which he had fine-combed his district for months, shaking hands, speechmaking at the drop of a hat or whisper of potential votes at every event from a dam dedication to a dogfight; and during which he had been driven to near distraction by constituents clamoring for attention, favors, jobs and the grinding of miscellaneous dull axes, had finally taken a night off back in Washington, D.C., celebrating in perhaps justifiable satisfaction until the small hours—falling into bed and immediate sweet slumber at 3 AM.

At 4 AM the telephone's resounding racket ended the Congressman's blissful but too brief respite. Half-asleep, half-sick and half-irritable he fumbled the phone to his ear, to hear the over-anxious, excited voice of a constituent a thousand miles distant, saying, "Congressman, I hate to wake you this time of night, but our Postmaster out here died a couple of hours ago and I'd like to take his place. I worked hard for you and figured maybe you would help me. Anyway, I'd like to take his place if it's OK with you."

To which our Congressman, still anxious to please, but cobwebby brained, made reply, "Sure, Bill, it's OK with me, if it's OK with the undertaker."

NOT FIRST CHOICE

In a hotly-contested race for the State Legislature, an incumbent member, realizing that he was involved in a tough battle for re-election, was making a strenuous effort in a door-to-door, street-by-street campaign.

Encountering a likely-looking prospective vote in the person of an obvious homeowner busily engaged in mowing his own lawn, our candidate introduced himself and developed what he happily felt to be a rather warm and friendly political conversation, which he in due time sought to terminate gracefully by remarking that he would appreciate the political support of his new acquaintance.

Somewhat to our candidate's surprise, the prospect said, "Well, I admire your spunk and you do seem to be sincere and a pretty friendly guy—but to be perfectly frank about it and not raise any false hopes, I have to tell you that you are *not* my first choice for the office."

Our candidate, thinking rapidly and still hopeful of salvaging a supporter, immediately replied, "I like your forthrightness and appreciate your frankness—and I heartily agree that the right to vote as one chooses is probably the most cherished and valuable of our inherited possessions. But you have deeply aroused my curiosity and I hope you will forgive me for inquiring as to who *is* your first choice?"

Our candidate's day was ruined by the prospect's apparently thoughtful and agonizingly slow response, "Well, let's see now -er -ah -well, dang near *anybody.*"

LOOKING FOR VOTES

Campaigning for public office in any district bordering the USA/Canada border has its own special difficulties. Witness the Montana northern border Legislative candidate working his way down the street, looking for votes.

Spotting a familiar-looking but unidentifiable chap, from dress and manner almost obviously a native cow-man-farmer, our candidate struck up a conversation and was soon much impressed at the scope of this voter's local acquaintance—his knowledge and grasp of current affairs, his obvious honesty, reliability, experience and—Oh Happy Day—apparent solid agreement with our candidate's political philosophy.

Well worth spending considerable precious campaign time on, our candidate decided, and did so, the better part of an hour elapsing before his new-found friend (and almost certainly valuable supporter) devastated our candidate's daydream by his adieu, "It's sure been a pleasure talking with you and I certainly hope you win the election. But I've got to get on my way home—it's a right smart piece to Xville (Canada) and crossing that line always takes extra time."

Mrs. Cynthia Newman
Republican National Committee, Virginia

SLEEP WITH THE PRESIDENT

The day of the 1948 election, Tom Dewey said to his wife, "I want you to go down and buy yourself a beautiful, filmy new nightie and negligee because tonight you are going to sleep with the President of the United States."

Mrs. Dewey did so, came home, donned her new nighttime finery, and sat down and waited, and waited, and waited.

Finally Tom came home, and looking sadly at his wife asked, "Well, aren't you going to say anything?"

"Just one thing," she replied. "Do I call Harry Truman or does he call me?"

Edmund E. Pendleton
Republican National Committee,
District of Columbia

MADISON AVENUE

I remember in the early days of closed circuit television the National Committee had arranged a large dinner program across the country for fund raising. The main event was in New York Madison Square Garden. I attended in Washington, and Joe Martin, House Leader, and a very popular Congressman, from Massachusetts, was presiding. On everyone's minds was the subject of public relations and the techniques used by the Madison Avenue advertising firms. When it reached the time for President Eisenhower to speak from New York, Joe Martin, carried away with the event, announced to our dinner crowd, "And now we take you to the great Madison Avenue spectacle in New York!" I think we missed the first five minutes of the President's speech as we all joined Joe in laughing over his mistake.

POLITICAL HANDSHAKE

It seems that the opposition candidate was doing too well. He was goodlooking and made a terrific impression when he was out "pressing the flesh." It seemed that all he would have to do to sweep the election was to continue attending receptions and shaking hands. Now it seems that the people discovered the alternate secret weapon, a man who had the unique talent of being able to throw up at will. The next day he joined the receiving line and waited to shake hands with the opposition candidate. When his turn came, and as he was shaking hands with the candidate, he had no difficulty in throwing up all over the candidate's most beautiful suit. From that day until the end of the campaign it was all downhill for the opposition candidate. Whenever he stood in the receiving line, his eyes inevitably were focused down the line to watch for the appearance of the horrible man with the trained stomach. Thus, as the candidate shook hands, he never looked at the person with whom he was shaking hands, but always down the line. His popularity fell and he was defeated.

Mrs. Elsa Sandstrom
Republican National Committee, California

SECRET

A secret is something you tell only one person at a time.

REAL LOSER

A real loser is the fellow who receives his junk mail with postage due.

TWO AIMS IN LIFE

One should have at least two aims in life: To make a little money first and then to make a little money last.

COLLEGE CAMPUS

Someone said that this year the college campuses could be so crowded that if a student wants a little solitude, he'll have to go to class.

EGOTIST

One good thing about an egotist: He never goes around talking about other people.

TEENAGE SON

Ad in local paper: "For sale: Complete set of encyclopedias, atlas, almanac and dictionary. Never used. Teenage son knows everything."

WORRY

The person who does not worry about the world situation these days should have his TV set examined.

DOGGIE BAG

Diner to waiter: "Please put the rest of my steak in a doggie bag—and put some bread in too, should the pup want to make a sandwich."

POLITICAL SCIENCE

Overheard: A father complaining that his son had just flunked political science—he never could tell his right from his left.

BLISTERS

Some people remind one of blisters. They never show up until the work is finished.

INFLATION

An inflation plus: The fellow who forgets his change nowadays doesn't lose anywhere near as much as he used to.

MEMORY

Another sign of getting on in years is when you finally find your glasses and then can't remember why you wanted them.

Bernard M. Shanley
Republican National Committee, New Jersey

CHURCHILL ON DE GAULLE

President Eisenhower had a tremendous sense of humor and I always recall his story of when he was appointed as the over-all Commander of Overlord for the invasion of France. Shortly after his appointment, Franklin Roosevelt and Churchill met with Stalin and returned to Casablanca, for a meeting on the invasion plans. President Eisenhower was called to this meeting and during the session, General DeGaulle was called before them as he was insistent on becoming the Commander of the French troops involved in the invasion. General Giriud, likewise wanted to command. After an impassioned plea to the group for his recommendation, General DeGaulle left. FDR turned to Churchill and said, "He really thinks he's Joan of Arc." Churchill replied, "Yes, but the Bishops won't let me burn him."

FAST EXIT

I recall Eisenhower's story of the early days in the African campaign, when he was to go on an inspection trip of installations along the coast. A young WAC was given the duty of driving him to these installations in a jeep. They started off and the General was in the back seat of the jeep. Finally, she turned to the General and said, "Do you mind if I stop?" He said not at all. She exited and shortly returned, and because of her confusion, jumped in, threw off the brakes, and started down the road. She went some distance and turned around, but there was no General in the back seat.

FIVE STAR MILKY WAY

During the same period, General Eisenhower needed a new pair of shoes, his having been worn out. It was raining hard and they stopped at a supply depot. A Sergeant was fitting the shoes, not realizing who General Eisenhower was. It became warm and the General took off his coat; the Sergeant looked up, saw the Five Stars, and said, "I don't believe it—it's the Milky Way!"

BOBBY CUTLER

Bobby Cutler was Director of the Security Council, and was scheduled to make a special appearance before the War College and return that night by plane, as we had a meeting the following morning of the National Security Council. As the meeting commenced, he started off with his speech, and the President interrupted him and said, having had a report from the War College, "Bobby, I hear you're quite a wit." Cutler said, "Are you sure that's what they say about me?"

Mrs. Oriette Sinclair
Republican National Committee, Idaho

POLITICIANS

Rare is the politician who can weigh the faults of his opponent without putting his thumb on the scales.

PUBLIC SPEAKING

A politician was told he was to begin his talk at a Rotary luncheon at 1:15 PM. He asked how long he should talk. "Talk as long as you'd like," was the reply. "We all leave at 1:30."

PLATFORM

The reason the Ten Commandments are clear and concise is that they weren't written by a Platform Committee.

IRS

Groundskeepers at one of the Federal Buildings were frustrated by pedestrians who were wearing a path across the lawn, completely ignoring the "Keep Off the Grass" signs. Finally, they posted a sign which was effective. It read, "Shortcut to IRS Office."

PUBLIC SPEAKING

When Peter J. Brennan was appointed Secretary of Labor, he was asked to describe his reaction to Washington and his new position. Brennan replied by telling the story of the young sheik whose father had just died. "When he was introduced to his late father's harem of about a hundred women, the son said, 'I know what is expected of me—but I don't know where to start.' "

GOVERNMENT

Christopher Columbus was responsible for the thinking of modern government. He didn't know where he was when he got there; and he did it all on borrowed money.

ELECTIONS

It's now clear how that fellow in Idaho got elected last year. In a survey he learned that there are more people belonging to minority groups than to majority groups. He realized that a majority of the minorities would have a plurality over a minority of the majorities, so he went after the minority vote and won a majority.

187

Charles A. Slocum
Republican National Committee, Minnesota

HUBERT HUMPHREY

Of course you've heard the story about the local Democratic-Farmer-Labor (DFL) chairman who purchased all of the available copies of Peter Benchley's book *Jaws* because he thought it was an autobiography of Hubert Humphrey?

ARAB IN IRELAND

Sometimes we Republicans feel we just can't do anything right. It reminds me of a story of a friend who was walking down the streets of Belfast, Northern Ireland, late one night. He was attacked and pulled into a dark alleyway—a knife placed at his throat. Asked in an Irish brogue, "What religion are ye?" it took only a short time to determine that this was not a winning proposition. After contemplating a second, he replied, "I'm Jewish," and waited, satisfied that he had been quite clever. Howling with delight, the attacker said, "Faith and b'gorry—I'm the luckiest Arab in Ireland!"

CAMPAIGN WAKE

Then there was the time that I was campaigning in Northern Minnesota with Clark MacGregor, a candidate for the U.S. Senate in 1970. Running a bit ahead of schedule, MacGregor asked that we stop in a small community near a church where he had spotted a crowd. MacGregor got out, greeted the people warmly and wished the bride and groom a joyous future. Several days later, he found himself in a similar situation and again ordered his driver to halt for a little spontaneous campaigning. It took the large Scottish Congressman only a few handshakes to determine that the people cared little

188

whether he was running for the U.S. Senate or not. Darkly clad, the people were mourning the death of a dear friend at a sad funeral. MacGregor never tried it a third time.

CHEAP SHOTS

After being charged as a political "cheap shot" artist by my DFL counterpart, I appeared on a forum with him in Northern Minnesota. In opening my statement, I alluded to the fact that my platform partner, the DFL State Chairman, had recently taken me to task because of my comments concerning certain top level DFL officials. I said that, after reviewing the spending policies of the DFL state administration and looking over Senator Humphrey's and Senator Mondale's recent voting records on fiscal matters, perhaps my comments were the only cheap things left in the state.

Estelle M. Stacy
Republican National Committee, Wyoming

HARD JOB

In a speech organized to develop enthusiasm in people who work for the Republican Party, I have often told this story:

A young man was madly in love with a charming young lady, but somehow could not get her to warm up to him. One night they were parked in a lovely spot overlooking the mountains. It was a beautiful moonlight night, and suddenly the young girl said, "You know, John, if we had the top down, I think I'd like to make love." The next day John was telling his friend about the incident, and the friend asked, "Well, how long did it take you to get the top down?" The young man replied, "It took eight minutes." "Eight minutes!" he replied, "my goodness alive, I can get the top of my car down in a minute and a half." "I know, but you have a convertible."

Then I add, "Don't put off a hard job. Use the same kind of enthusiasm displayed by this young man, and get right to work to achieve your objective."

HEAD STRAIGHT

When I feel Republicans are not thinking straight, I often tell this story:

One winter day, two men were riding along on a motorcycle. The one in back had lost the buttons off his coat and he was about to freeze. He had the driver stop so he could put the coat on backwards; then as they rode along, the coat pressed against him and offered protection from the cold wind. Suddenly a truck came off a side road and smashed into the motorcycle. The next day, a

190

patrolman was telling his friend about the accident. He said, "You know the driver of the motorcycle was dead when we got to the scene of the accident. The man riding behind was alive when we got there, but after we got his head straightened around, he died."

I have used this to admonish Republicans to keep their heads on straight.

STREAKING

There was a little old lady in a nursing home who had become bored with the situation, so she decided she would go out and streak the lounge to stir up a little excitement. She takes off all her duds, and parades into the lounge. There were two little old men sitting over against the wall; one said to the other, "Did you see that woman pass here?" "Yes, but what was that she had on?" "I don't know, but whatever it was, it sure needed ironing."

COMMITTEE

I often define a committee this way: The unwilling, recruited from the unfit, to do the unnecessary.

SUNDAY SCHOOL

A man's son was telling his family about his Sunday School lesson: "Moses crossing the Red Sea."

"Moses had his engineers build a pontoon bridge across the sea," he said. "Then his people crossed it. Then his reconnaisance planes radioed and told him an Egyptian tank corps was about to cross the bridge, too. So Moses ordered his jets to blow up the bridge. They did. So Moses and his people were safe."

"Are you sure that's how your Sunday School teacher told the story?" asked his father.

"Well, not really," admitted the son. "But the way she told it .. you just wouldn't believe it!"

Acknowledgements

This book of Republican Humor is intended to introduce a bit of levity into the political arena.

President Gerald R. Ford, Vice President Nelson A. Rockefeller, members of the Cabinet, Republican members of Congress, Governors, Ambassadors, members of the Republican National Committee and other prominent Republicans contributed the material. The editors are happy to present their favorite jokes, anecdotes and cartoons for your reading pleasure.

Working many hours with the editors to bring this book to the readers were Jane and David Duperrault, Jan Gregoire and Marguerite Porter. Their assistance was invaluable.

To Eddie Mahe, Jr., Executive Director of the Republican National Committee, we owe special thanks, for he gave the initial impetus that made this book possible. And to Bruce McBrearty of the Republican National Finance Committee for his help, we say, well done and much thanks.

To Jack Calkins, of the White House, and Joe Persico of the office of the Vice President, we are most grateful for their wonderful cooperation.

For photography we are grateful to David Hume Kennerly of the White House, and Elizabeth Harrison of the Republican National Committee.

And to Mary Louise Smith, Chairman of the Republican National Committee, for her full support of our effort, we are most appreciative.

May all who read this book find as much reading pleasure as did the editors in putting it together.

Steve Skubik, Editor
Hal E. Short, Co-editor

A

"Absent Minded," 94
Acknowledgement, 192
"Adam and Eve," 67
Adams, Don W., 154
"Advertising," 45
"Advice to the Lovelorn," 123
Akins, James E., 48
"Alaska," 56
"Alben Barkley's Speech," 163
Albert, Carl, 137
Ali, Muhammed, 129
Allen, John, 84
"American History," 128
"American Indian," 118
Anderson, Jack, 82
"Angels," 87
"Answers," 33
"Anybody up There?", 80
"Appropriation," 17
"Arab in Ireland," 188
Archer, Bill, 100
Ashbrook, John M., 101
Austad, Mark Evans, 49
"Autograph," 65

B

"Bad Bills," 63
"Bad Luck," 44
Banowsky, Bill, 35
Barber, Miller, 14
Barkley, Alben, 163
Barrett, Concepcion, 158
Barton, Mrs. Harold B., 157
"Battle of the Sexes," 15
Beame, Abe, 19
"Beauty and Charm," 157
"Bed Fellows," 50
Benchley, Peter, 188
Bennett, Robert F., 53
"Benny, Jack," 88
"Better Mousetrap," 135
Biebel, Frederick K., 155
Bilbo, Theodore G, 83, 84
"Blisters," 183
Boren, James, 113
"Boring," 121
Boulton, Grace, 159
Bowen, Otis R., 54
"Boy Scouts," 17
Brennan, Edward, 160
Brennan, Peter J., 186
Brewer, Myrene R., 161
Brock, Bill, 69

"Broken Arm," 121
Broom, Bill, 20
"Brother Lion," 114
Brown, Clarence, 103
Bryant, Bear, 18, 19
Buckley, Bill, 109
Buckley, Jim, 8, 108, 109
"Budget," 22
Burch, Dean, 42
"Burglars," 140
Bush, George, 22, 40
Butler, Amon, 68

C

"Cab Driver," 165
"Cabinet Highjinks," 47
Calkins, Jack, 192
"Call Girl," 158
"Campaign School," 111
"Campaign Slogan," 89
"Campaign Wake," 188
"Career," 71
Cargo, David F., 62
Carlin, George, 23
Cartwright, Peter, 113
"Changing Parties," 132
"Cheap Shots," 189
"Chin Up," 44
Christopher Columbus, 187
"Churchill on DeGaulle," 184
Churchill, Winston, 128, 184
"C.I.A.," 37
Clements, Bill, 34
Cleveland, Grover, 140
Cohen, William S. 104
"College Campus," 182
Collins, James M., 105
"Committee," 191
"Communications," 32, 33
"Conference," 135
"Confusion," 53
"Congress in Recess," 125
"Congressional Esteem," 162
"Congressman," 141
"Conservatism," 82
Conte, Silvio O., 106
Cooper, John Sherman, 51
"Cosell, Howard," 18, 19
"Cow Stealing," 73
Cramer, William C., 162
"Crying," 50
Curtis, Carl T., 71
Cutler, Bobby, 185

D

Daley, Richard, 145
"Dancing," 16
"David Mathews," 31, 32
Davis, Stuart, 33
"Deciding Vote," 79
"Decision," 137
"Democrats," 6, 8, 90, 124
Derwinski, Edward J., 108
Devine, Sam, 24
Dewey, George, 126
Dewey, Tom, 179
"Diego Garcia," 91
"Die Happy," 161
"Different View," 18
"Diplomacy," 140
Dirksen, Everett, 134, 145
"Dogs," 15, 127, 165
"Doggie Bag," 183
Dole, Bob, 73
Domenici, Pete V., 75
Donnelly, Rubin H., 49
Dorsey, Tommy, 16
"Driver's Seat," 53
"Drum," 45
Duperrault, David, 192
Duperrault, Jane, 192

E

"Egotist," 182
Eisenhower, Dwight, 180, 184, 185
"Election Returns," 129
"Elections," 187
"Emancipation Proclamation," 39
"Energy Crisis," 38
"Epitaph," 154
Esch, Marvin L., 111
Eshleman, Edwin D., 112
"Ethics," 160
"Ex-Congressmen," 28
"Executive," 105
"Exposure," 124
"Extremism," 81

F

Fannin, Bobby, 78
Fannin, Paul J., 77, 167
"Farmer," 55, 83, 134
"Fast Exit," 184
"Fat Man's Party," 113
"Fear," 125
"Federal Government," 140
Ferrell, Don, 159
Findley, Paul, 113

"First Vote," 161
"Fish," 58
"Five Star Milky Way," 185
"Football," 13, 18, 19, 23
Ford, Betty, 16, 29, 32, 115
"Ford Foundation," 37
Ford, Gerald R., 7, 8, 13, 18, 19, 27, 28, 33, 37, 53, 192
Ford, Henry, 104
"Ford-Mustang," 34
Ford, Susan, 15, 16, 29
"Foreign Aid," 65
Forward, David R., 164
"Forty Nine Minute Week," 90
Frame, Richard C., 165
"Fresh Air," 85
"Friends," 40, 162
Fulbright, J. William, 73
"Fund Raising," 27, 45, 105

G
Garn, Jake, 79
"George Washington," 99
Georgine, Bob, 36
Getty, J. Paul, 56
Gibran, Kahlil, 7
Ginn, Mrs. M. Stanley, 166
"Gin Rummy," 35
Ginsburg, Sol, 114
Godwin, Mills E., Jr., 55
"Going to Hell," 113
Goldwater, Barry, 37, 42, 81, 89, 167
"Goldy Bearwater," 42
"Golf," 13
"Goodbye God," 126
"Good Candidate—But," 168
"Good Enough," 149
"Gorilla," 125
"Government," 187
"Government Relations," 128
"Government Spending," 103, 167
"Great Americans," 40
Gregoire, Jan, 192
Gude, Gilbert, 114
Guyer, Tennyson, 116

H
Hammond, Jay S., 56
"Hang One," 159
"Hard Job," 190
"Hardware Store," 32
Harrison, Elizabeth, 192
Hartke, Vance, 74
Haugh, John H., 167
Hayes, Woody, 19, 20
"Head Straight," 190
Heinz, H. John, III, 118
Herman, Woody, 16
"Higher Office," 90
Hills, Carla, 25
Hogan, Ben, 13, 14
Holt, Marjorie S., 119
Holton Arms School, 29
Hooper, Mrs. James F., 168
Hoover, Herbert, 149
Hope, Bob, 19, 23, 25, 31
"Hot Air," 32
"How to Lose Friends," 145

"How to Win Elections," 145
Hruska, Roman L., 83
Humphrey, Hubert, 8, 21, 23, 63, 74, 121, 129, 188, 189
Hyde, Henry J., 121

I
"Identity," 131, 167
"Identity Problem," 101
"I'm a Territorial," 158
"Impression," 61
"Inflation," 182
"Instant Deflation," 85
"Instructions," 122
"Introduction," 61
"Issues and Answers," 94
"Italian Representation," 76
"It's a Tough Life," 164

J
Jackson, Scoop, 21, 25, 26
Johnson, Don, 28
Johnson, James P., 122
Johnson, Lyndon, 145
Johnson, Robert E., Cadet, 28
Joly, Cyril M., Jr., 170
"Juror," 96

K
"Kansas," 22
Karsh, Yousef, 109
Kendziorski, Casimir, 64
Kennedy, John, 69
Kennedy, Teddy, 82
Kennerly, David Hume, 15, 16, 192
"Kentucky Colonel," 46
"Kentucky Politician," 175
"Kind Words," 49
"King Caucus," 137
Kissinger, Henry, 14, 15, 17, 26, 33, 34, 47
"Kittens," 88
Kleppe, Thomas S., 44
Knowles, Warren P., 64

L
Lagomarsino, Robert J., 123
Landers, Ann, 123
"Last Laugh," 115
"Laugh-in," 108
Laxalt, Paul, 85
Levine, Norman, 35
"Liar," 146
"Life's Little Apples," 115
"Likee Speechee?", 152
Lincoln, Abraham, 39, 113, 119, 146
Linnell, John R., 171
"Lion's Cage," 143
"Lobbying," 112
"Long Winded," 74, 101
"Looking for Votes," 177
Lorge, Gerald D., 64
"Love," 55

M
MacGregor, Clark, 188
"Making Money," 162

"Malaprops," 64
"Man of Caliber," 50
Mannek, Reimund, 103
"Marbles," 52
"Marriage," 83
Martin, Joe, 180
Mathews, David, 31, 32
Mathias, Charles McC., Jr., 87
McClory, Robert, 124
McGovern, George, 73
McKay, John, 19, 20
McMath, George N., 173
Meany, George, 137
Meir, Golda, 82
"Memory," 116, 183
"Memory Tax," 73
Michalski, Clem, 64
"Microphone," 155
Middleton, Edwin C., 175
Milbank, Jeremiah, 43
Milland, Ray, 65
Miller, Vern, 53
Millican, Tom, 40
Milliken, William G., 58
Mitchell, Jim, 25
Moberly, Mrs. Isabel C., 176
Mondale, Senator, 189
Moore, Arch A., 59
Moore, W. Henson, 125
Moorehead, Carlos J., 126
Morton, Rogers C.B., 44, 45, 46, 47, 132
Morton, Truston, 45
"Mousetrap," 67
"Move Fast," 59
"Mr. Devil," 139
"Mr. President," 37
"Music," 30, 71

N
"Name Card," 46
"Nazi Soldier," 121
Nelson, Byron, 13, 14
"Nervous," 52
"Nervous Breakdown," 141
Nessen, Ron, 15, 26
"New Dealer," 147
Newman, Cynthia, 179
Nicklaus, Jack, 13, 14
"Nightmare," 73
"Nineteen Eighty Four," 62
"Noah's Ark," 50
"No Condition to Travel," 50
"Not First Choice," 176
"Nutty Legislation," 106

O
"Obstructionists," 91
"Ode to the Welfare State," 170
"Oldest Profession," 67
"On the Floor?", 129
"Open Mouth," 124
"Outside of Lock 77," 151

P
Packwood, Bob, 88
Palmer, Arnold, 13, 14
Parseghian, Ara, 19

Pendleton, Ned, 180
Percy, Charles H. 89
Perez, Peter, 158
Persico, Joe, 192
"Persuasion," 93
"Ph.D," 77
"Photogenic," 109
"Pismire," 91
"Platform," 186
"Player, Gary, 14
"Politician(s)," 28, 55, 89, 92,
   116, 124, 127, 186
"Political Advertising," 93
"Political Favors," 83
"Political Handshake," 180
"Political Science," 183
"Political Truth," 115
"Politics," 105, 116
"Polls," 58
Pond, Ducky, 19
Pope John XXIII, 109, 113
Porter, Marguerite, 192
"Post Script," 51
"Prayer," 82
"Pray for People," 161
"Presidential Candidate," 126
"Presidential Candidates," 21, 25,
   26, 27
"Presidents," 17, 20
"Press, The," 14
"Press Interviews," 39
Pressler, Larry, 127
"Press Lightly," 51
Prichard, John, 64
Prince Faisal, 48
"Prison Speech," 97
"Professionals," 142
"Prohibition," 48
"Promises," 121
"Psychiatrist," 40
"Public Ethics," 104
"Public Speaking," 29, 137, 186
"Put Down," 75

Q
"Question of Legs, The," 119
"Quick Fun," 130

R
Ray, Robert D., 61
Reagan, Nancy, 65, 66
Reagan, Ronald, 65, 69, 81
"Real Loser," 182
"Receptionist," 68
Reed, John, 52
"Registration," 16
"Republican Party," 37
"Republicans Try Harder," 90
"Responsibilities," 37
Rhodes, John J., 128
Rice, Grantland, 19
Rinaldo, Matthew J., 129
" 'Rip' Whalen," 31
"Rivalry," 114
"Road Directions," 59, 171
Rockefeller, John D., 50
Rockefeller, Nelson, 9, 30, 33,
   37, 124, 192

Rogers, Will, 135
Rooney, John, 17
Roosevelt, Franklin, 184
"Run Giovani," 109
Ruppe, Phil, 145
Ruth, Earl B., 68

S
"Saint Peter," 79
Sandstrom, Elsa, 182
Sarazen, Gene, 14
Sawyer, Grant, 85
Schenkel, Chris, 18
Schneebeli, Herman T., 131
"School Girl," 148
Schulze, Richard T., 132
Scott, Hugh, 90
Scott, Walter, 8
Scott, William L., 92
Sebelius, Keith G., 134
"Secret," 182
"Security," 66
"Self Made Men," 82
"Senior Prom," 29
"Sex," 82
"Sexual Discrimination," 15
Shanley, Bernard, 184
Sheehan, Bishop, 50
Shuster, E. G. "Bud," 135
Shuttleworth, Barbara, 21
Simon, Bill, 30
"Sin," 70
Sinclair, Oriette, 186
Skubitz, Joe, 137
"Sleep With the President," 179
Slocum, Charles A., 188
"Small Businessman," 30
"Small Town," 49
Smith, Homer, 28, 29
Smith, Mary Louise, 25, 39, 41, 192
Snead, Sam, 14
"Sneaking Suspicions," 50
"Sober Reappraisal," 62
"Socialism," 128
"Sorry," 77
"Southern Democrats," 99
"Speech Writer," 100
"Spence, Floyd, 139
Stacy, Estelle M., 190
Stafford, Robert T., 93
Stalin, 184
"Stay Alive," 123
Steelman, Alan, 140
Stevens, Ted, 27
Stockton, Dave, 14
Strauss, Bob, 25, 26, 27, 40
"Streaking," 191
"Sunday School," 191
"Surfing," 35
Sussman, Norman, 64
Symms, Steve, 142

T
Taft, Robert, Jr., 94
Taft, William Howard, 95
"Tail Gunner," 120
"Take it All," 171
"Tax Collector," 149

Taylor, Gene, 143
"Teenage Son," 182
"Telephone," 20, 82
"Telephone Conversation," 176
"Tell Your Side," 77
Temple, Shirley, 63
Terra, Dan, 17
"Texas Outhouse," 49
"The Candidate," 81
"The Common Man," 83
"The Goose Issue," 69
"The 94th (Congress) Psalm," 149
"The Word," 62
Thomas, Helen, 15
Thorsness, Leo, 15
Thurmond, Strom, 96
"Toastmaster," 88, 155
Tower, John G., 99
"Town Idiot," 96
Trinke, William, 64
"Truck Driver," 54
Truman, Harry, 22, 88, 179
"Truth," 100
Tuck, William M., 55
"T.V. Newscasters," 26
"Twenty Two Gun Salute," 121
"Two Aims in Life," 182
"225,000 Letters," 49
"Two More Questions," 77
"Two Party System," 81, 168

U
"Under Oath," 53
"Unemployed," 140

V
"Vaccinated," 120
Vander Jagt, Guy, 145
Volpe, John A. 52
"Vos Omnes," 90
"Vote Right," 69

W
Wadsworth, George, 48
"Waiter," 155
Wallace, George, 109
"Washington, D.C.," 140
Washington, George, 99
Watson, Jim, 40
Weiskopf, Tom, 14
Welch, Raquel, 28, 29
"Welfare Department Letters," 173
Wepner, Chuck, 129
"When in Doubt," 114
"White House, The," 37
Whitehurst, G. William, 147
"Who's That," 92
Williams, John Sharp, 83
"Will Rogers," 135
Winn, Larry, 148
"Women," 166
"Women in Politics," 157
"Worry," 183
"Wrong Decision," 75
Wydler, John W., 149
Wylie, Chalmers P., 151

Y
Young, C. W. Bill, 152